50 Great Walks in

BRITAIN

Handpicked for Dog Owners

Published by AA Publishing a trading name of Automobile Association Developments Limited, whose registered office is Fanum House, Basing View, Basingstoke, Hampshire RG21 4EA. Registered number 1878835.

ISBN-10: 0-7495-4023-0
ISBN-13: 978-0-7495-4023-4

A04073

© Automobile Association Developments Limited 2003
Illustrations © Automobile Association Developments Limited 2003
This collection first published 2003, reprinted in 2006 & 2009 as part of Great Dog Walks kit. The contents of this book are drawn from material previously published by AA Publishing.

Enabled by [Ordnance Survey] This product includes mapping data licensed from Ordnance Survey® with the permission of the Controller of Her Majesty's Stationery Office. © Crown copyright 2009. All rights reserved. Licence number 1000021153

Visit AA Publishing at www.theAA.com/bookshop

Packaged exclusively on behalf of the AA by Top That! Publishing plc.
Printed and bound in China.
Front cover: Getty Images.
For more information about aqua3 maps visit www.aqua3.com

Legend

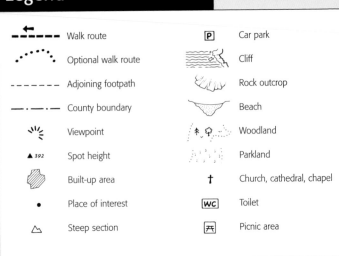

▬ ▬ ◄ ▬ ▬	Walk route	P	Car park
••••••	Optional walk route		Cliff
▬ ▬ ▬ ▬ ▬	Adjoining footpath		Rock outcrop
▬ · ▬ · ▬	County boundary		Beach
☀	Viewpoint	♠ ♧	Woodland
▲ 392	Spot height		Parkland
	Built-up area	†	Church, cathedral, chapel
•	Place of interest	WC	Toilet
△	Steep section	⊼	Picnic area

Britain locator map

Thurso

Ullapool

Inverness

SCOTLAND

Aberdeen

Fort William
50
49
48

Perth

47

Edinburgh
43

Glasgow
45
44
Berwick-upon-Tweed

Ayr

41
40

46
Dumfries

42

Newcastle upon Tyne

Carlisle

39
38
Middlesbrough

Kendal
NORTH
36
Scarborough

37
York

Blackpool
33
Leeds
Kingston upon Hull

34
35

Liverpool
Manchester
Sheffield

Holyhead
Chester
32
18
Lincoln

29
28
19
20

30
31
Nottingham
Norwich

Shrewsbury
21
Leicester
EAST

25
23
22
Peterborough
17

Aberystwyth
24
Birmingham
Cambridge

WALES
CENTRAL
Worcester
Luton
Ipswich

26
Carmarthen
Gloucester
15
16

Swansea
7
Swindon
LONDON
Southend-
on-Sea

27
Cardiff
Bristol
10
Reading
11
SOUTH
14

Barnstaple
8
9
Guildford
13
EAST
Dover

SOUTH WEST
6
Portsmouth
12
Eastbourne

3
Exeter

2
4
Bournemouth

Truro
Plymouth
5

Contents

Contents

WALK		RATING	DISTANCE	PAGE

Rating: These walks have been selected to offer dog walkers a wide range of environments and landscapes. Difficulties such as stiles and roads have been avoided, where possible. Each walk has been rated for its relative difficulty compared to the other walks in this book. Walks marked ⬛ are likely to be shorter and easier with little total ascent. The hardest walks are marked ◣.

Walking in Safety: For advice and safety tips see page 128.

Walking the Dog

Writer and experienced Jack Russell walker Ann F Stonehouse shares a few aspects of dog lore to help you enjoy these walks.

The world of walking, it seems, is divided into people who hike for a hobby and those of us who need the excuse of taking our dog for a walk to drag us from the comfort of our armchairs. And at last here's a practical walking book specially created for those of us who think that a country walk without a canine companion is only half the fun (if not, indeed, pointless).

There are 50 great, mostly circular, walks here, spread out across England, Scotland and Wales, that you can enjoy together. Many are mapped and all give details of the relevant Ordnance Survey maps that will help to keep you on the right track.

These walks have been carefully selected for their interest and scenic beauty, but more especially for their general dog friendliness. For example, as well as giving advice about parking,

we've picked start points where an excited hound jumping out of a vehicle, eager for the off, won't bounce straight into the traffic. And the routes vary from 2 to 10 miles (3.2km to 16.1km) in length, which should suit most dogs as well as their owners. None of the walks is through particularly tough terrain so you don't need to be super-fit, but a grading system of pawprints suggests difficulty on a scale of one to three, and there's a gradient figure to show just how much uphill climbing is involved in each walk.

In many cases, we've been able to choose routes that are enclosed in some way. This might be an old railway line, a fenced path, beach or woodland where you can let your dog run freely. But still always consider the local wildlife and other folk who may be sharing the path. On many stretches, it's best to keep your dog under careful control. It's not always possible to avoid roads, but we've done our best to keep to the quiet lanes and byways.

Many of the walks cross farmland where livestock may be grazing and a lead is essential. In my experience, responsible dog owners are well aware of the need to avoid disturbing farm animals, but sometimes it seems that the beasts could do with a code themselves. Let's face it, being encircled by curious bullocks, nudged by nosy horses, and even chased across bare hilltops by sheep who think you've come to feed them can be unnerving experiences (and in the case of the sheep, very embarrassing for the Jack Russell concerned).

PUBLIC TRANSPORT ⓘ

Access by public transport to some of the more rural parts of Britain can be a challenge, but it's well worth a try (and one of these walks starts from a railway station). In many of the National Parks you will find services specially geared for walkers. For timetable information much of the country is now included on the Traveline service. You can call it on 0871 200 2223 or seek out their website – www.traveline.org.uk. Dogs generally travel free on trains, but may have to pay a nominal fee on some buses.

We've even tried to select routes that are not broken up by too many stiles – any walker who's had to struggle repeatedly over awkward field boundaries, clutching their wet, muddy, wriggling pet, will appreciate this. There are recommendations of what to look out for along the way, and suggested places of refreshment near by. Many of these actively welcome dogs as well as their owners, but it's always advisable to ask before you both walk in, as house rules vary. Some landlords may hand out pats, dog treats and water bowls while they keep you waiting for your beer, but other establishments prefer a more low-key approach. Generally, a well-behaved dog sitting quietly under a table is unlikely to cause offence.

So if you and your dog are looking for somewhere for walkies this weekend, we hope you find something here to tempt you both. For somewhere dog-friendly to stay, why not consult the *AA Pet Friendly Places to Stay* guide, or check the web at www.theAA.com.

Enjoy your walk!

Using this Book

Information panels

An information panel for each walk shows its relative difficulty (page 5), the distance and total amount of ascent. An indication of the gradients you will encounter is shown by the rating ▲▲▲ (no steep slopes) to ▲▲▲ (several very steep slopes).

Maps

There are 30 maps, covering 40 of the walks. Some walks have a suggested option in the same area. The information panel for these walks will tell you how much extra walking is involved. On short-cut suggestions the panel will tell you the total distance if you set out from the start of the main walk. Where an option returns to the same point on the main walk, just the distance of the loop is given. Where an option leaves the main walk at one point and returns to it at another, then the distance shown is for the whole walk. The minimum time suggested is for reasonably fit walkers and doesn't allow for stops. Each walk has a suggested map. Laminated aqua3 maps are longer lasting and water resistant.

Start Points

The start of each walk is given as a six-figure grid reference prefixed by two letters indicating which 100km square of the National Grid it refers to. You'll find more information on grid references on most Ordnance Survey maps.

Dogs

Please respect other countryside users. Keep your dog under control, especially around livestock, and obey local bylaws and other dog control notices. For more information see the dog walker's code on page 128.

Car Parking

Many of the car parks suggested are public, but occasionally you may find you have to park on the roadside or in a lay-by. Please be considerate when you leave your car, ensuring that access roads or gates are not blocked and that other vehicles can pass safely. Remember that pub car parks are private and should not be used unless you have the owner's permission.

A Walk Through the Bishop's Wood

A short and gentle stroll through the richly diverse woodlands of a forestry estate near Truro.

•DISTANCE•	3½ miles (5.7km)
•MINIMUM TIME•	2hrs 30min
•ASCENT / GRADIENT•	164ft (50m) ▲ ▲ ▲
•LEVEL OF DIFFICULTY•	
•PATHS•	Forest tracks and paths. Can be very muddy after rain
•LANDSCAPE•	Mixed woodland
•SUGGESTED MAP•	aqua3 OS Explorer 105 Falmouth & Mevagissey
•START / FINISH•	Grid reference: SW 820477
•DOG FRIENDLINESS•	Dogs are welcomed throughout woods. The authorities ask that owners clear up their dog's mess in car park and first sections of forest tracks
•PARKING•	Forestry car park, north of Idless, near Truro
•PUBLIC TOILETS•	None on route
•NOTE•	Car park gates are closed at sunset. Working woodland, please heed notices advising work in progress

BACKGROUND TO THE WALK

Going down to the woods in Cornwall is always a delightful antidote to the county's surfeit of sea. Coastal woodlands do not always offer such an escape; views of the sea, the sound of the sea, and even the smell of the sea keep intruding. At leafy enclaves such as Bishop's Wood near Truro, however, you can safely bury the anchor deep inland. Bishop's Wood is a part of the much larger St Clement Woods that lie a few miles north of Truro and just north of the village of Idless. It acquired its name from the time it was owned by the Bishop of Exeter during the late medieval period. Long before this, probably when the ancient woodland of the area had already been stripped bare by the early farmers, the highest point of the wood was crowned by a fortified Iron-Age settlement from which the surrounding countryside could be easily viewed.

Woodland Industry

Today, the substantial banks of the settlement survive, muffled by dense woodland cover. In later centuries, when tree cover was re-established here, the area would have been a typical working woodland. The mix of broad-leaved trees that makes up much of the area indicates long-established forestry. The Iron-Age site is densely covered with coppiced oaks. You can identify them by their multiple trunks at the base. When the woods were actively managed for coppicing, the trunks would be cut so that new growth started in several places at once. They would be allowed to grow like this for up to 20 years or so before being harvested for charcoal making, basket making or a host of other wood products. Up to the beginning of the 20th century many woods were managed in this way. The practice is being re-introduced in some areas in Cornwall, because of its beneficial effects on wildlife habitats.

Eerie Track

The walk starts from the excellent forestry car park at the south end of the woods and leads along its eastern edge through Lady's Wood, on a track that feels wonderfully eerie and enclosed. A robust little stream, a tributary of the River Allen, runs below the track. Beech trees dominate the cover here and, further into the wood, oak, hazel, birch, Japanese larch and holly can be seen standing either side of the track. In the springtime the trees are bright with fresh leaves; the soft yellow and cream hazel and willow catkins are dusted with pollen and the rich earth beneath the trees supports a wealth of plants, ferns and mosses. Look particularly for wood sorrel, bluebells, three-cornered leeks, and the feathery fronds of male ferns.

The track leads on to the top end of the wood just before Lanner Mill. Here you turn uphill and on to a broad forestry ride that leads back south along the higher ridge of the woods. Halfway along you can divert left from the track to visit the site of the Iron-Age settlement. The large bank and ditch that encircled the site is still visible. The rigid upper branches of the numerous coppiced oak trees enclose the central trunks of the trees like cages. This is a well-preserved site although the tree growth and associated scrub blur the full impact of the very large bank and ditch construction. Such hilltop sites date from the transition between the Bronze Age and Iron Age and reflect a growing territorialism amongst early Britons.

Walk 1

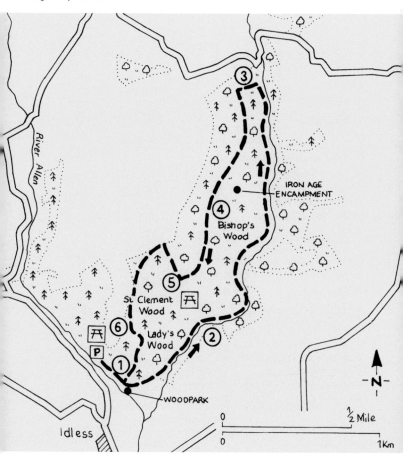

Walk 1

Commercial Centres

These were not forts in the narrow sense of being built purely for defence. They were defensible sites, certainly, but they were commercial and cultural centres as much as anything else, being the focus of a large territory of scattered farmsteads and settlements from which the unforested hilltop site would be easily seen. The hilltop 'fort' or 'castle' represented a central refuge in times of trouble, but served also as a place to bring livestock to market and to exchange household goods and to socialise and celebrate. From the Iron-Age site, the last part of the walk takes you on to even higher ground and through newly planted conifers; the young trees are still low enough to afford a distant glimpse of the elegant spires of Truro's cathedral, a fitting view from a Bishop's Wood.

Walk 1 Directions

① Leave the top end of the car park via the wooden barrier and go along a broad track. In a few paces, at a fork, keep to the right fork and follow the track above **Woodpark** and along the inside edge of the wood. This track can be very muddy after rain.

② Keep on the main track, parallel to the river, ignoring branch tracks leading off to the left.

③ Just before the northern end of the wood reach a fork. Keep to the main track as it bends left and uphill. The track levels off and at an open area merges with a broad forestry ride. Keep ahead along this ride.

④ At a forestry notice indicating the site of the remains of an **Iron-Age encampment**, go left along a path beneath conifer trees to reach the bank and ditch of the encampment. Return to the main track and turn left.

⑤ At a bend beside a wooden bench, where tracks lead off to left and right, go right and follow a public footpath uphill. At a path crossing turn left and follow the path through scrubland and young pine trees.

> **WHAT TO LOOK FOR** ⓘ
> Old woods are often rich in **fungi**. Look for the trunks of dead trees and you may find the great plate-like layers of various bracket fungi. Other fungi to look for among the rich humus of the woodland underlayer are stinkhorn fungus, the rudely unmistakable *Phallus impudicus*. On oak trees you may find little round wood-like growths known popularly as 'oak apples'. These are produced by gall wasps laying their eggs on oak leaves. The oak apple grows round the egg to protect it during incubation. Look closely and you may see a tiny hole where the adult insect has emerged.

> **WHERE TO EAT AND DRINK** ⓘ
> There are no food and drink outlets on the walk and the immediate area is quite isolated; but **Truro** is only a few miles away and there is a pub at **Shortlanesend** about 1 mile (1.6km) to the west of Idless.

⑥ Re-enter mature woodland and follow a track downhill. Keep right at a junction, then go left at the next junction. Reach a T-junction with a broad track. Turn right and follow the track to the **car park**.

Princetown: Thomas Tyrwhitt's Dream

There was great industrial activity here in the late 18th and early 19th centuries, but it's still the middle of nowhere!

•DISTANCE•	7 miles (11.3km)
•MINIMUM TIME•	3hrs
•ASCENT / GRADIENT•	328ft (100m) ▲ ▲ ▲
•LEVEL OF DIFFICULTY•	
•PATHS•	Tracks, leat-side paths and rough moorland
•LANDSCAPE•	Open moorland
•SUGGESTED MAP•	aqua3 OS Explorer OL28 Dartmoor
•START / FINISH•	Grid reference: SX 588735
•DOG FRIENDLINESS•	Can be off lead at all times, but watch for sheep
•PARKING•	Main car park in Princetown (honesty box)
•PUBLIC TOILETS•	By car park

BACKGROUND TO THE WALK

Even on a summer's day, when fluffy clouds scud across a blue sky and the high moor looks particularly lovely, Princetown is bleak. There's nothing soft and gentle about the place – most of the buildings are functional in the extreme, uncompromising, grey and harsh. The town, 1,395ft (425m) above sea level, and with an average annual rainfall of 82in (2,160mm), was founded by Sir Thomas Tyrwhitt in the late 18th century, and named in honour of the Prince Regent, to whom he was both a friend and private secretary.

Dartmoor Prison

Tyrwhitt persuaded the government to build a prison here for French prisoners from the Napoleonic wars. Building work started in 1806, and the first prisoners were in situ by 1809, joined by Americans in 1813. At one time 7,000 men were held. Closed in 1813, the prison reopened in 1850 as a civilian establishment, which it remains to this day – a monumental building, best seen from the Two Bridges to Tavistock road, to the north of the town.

There is mention of the ancient landmark of Nun's Cross (or Siward's Cross) as early as 1280, in documents concerning ownership of Buckland Abbey lands. Over 7ft (2.1m) high, it stands on the route of the Abbot's Way – between Buckfast Abbey and Tavistock – and marks the eastern boundary of Buckland Abbey lands. The word 'Siward' engraved on its eastern face may refer to the Earl of Northumberland who owned much land in this part of the country in Saxon times, or may indicate some connection to a family named Siward who lived near by. 'Bocland' on the other face may be a reference to Buckland Abbey. The word 'Nun's' comes from the Celtic *nans*, meaning combe or valley.

The Devonport Leat is an amazing feat of engineering, carried out between 1793 and 1801 to improve water supplies to Devonport, now part of Plymouth, which at that time was being developed as a naval base. Originally 26½ miles (43km) long, it carried 2 million gallons (4.5 million litres) of water a day. Lined with granite slabs and conveying crystal-clear, fast-flowing water, today it provides an extremely attractive, level walking route through some otherwise fairly inhospitable terrain. The final part of the walk, back to Princetown, follows the abandoned railway track that Tyrwhitt planned to link Princetown with Plymouth. The line, the first iron railway in the county, opened in 1823. More of a tramway than a railway, the horse-drawn wagons carried coal and lime up from Plymouth, and took stone back. In 1881 commercial considerations caused the line to be taken over by the Princetown Railway Company. It reopened as a steam railway in 1883, until its eventual closure in 1956.

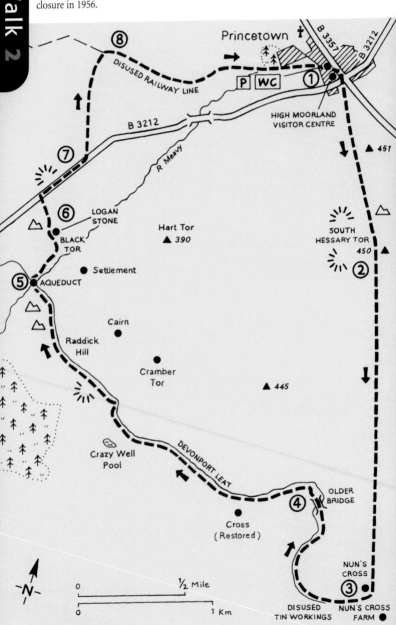

Walk **2**

Walk 2 Directions

① Leave the car park past the toilets and turn right to pass the **High Moorland Visitor Centre**. Cross the road and follow the lane between the two pubs and their car parks behind. After 100yds (91m) a small gate leads to a broad gravelly track which ascends gently to **South Hessary Tor**, from which there are splendid views to **Plymouth Sound** ahead, and of the prison behind.

WHERE TO EAT AND DRINK   ⓘ

The **Plume of Feathers** inn, originally a coaching house, is the oldest building in Princetown, dating from 1785. It has a campsite and camping barn and is a popular stopover for those exploring the moor on foot. Nearby is the **Railway Inn**. Both pubs are free houses, welcome families and serve good food.

---

② Follow the track as it drops down gently, passing boundary stones. It crosses two other tracks (look left for a view of the **Devonport Leat**) before dropping down to **Nun's Cross**. **Nun's Cross Farm** (originally a thatched house, c 1870) can be seen to the left.

③ Turn 90 degrees right at the cross to pick your way over a bumpy area of disused tin workings to find the end of the tunnel where the leat emerges. It's near the remains of a cottage under a beech and three hawthorn trees. Walk along the right bank of the leat.

④ Where the leat bends north cross it on **Older Bridge** (granite slabs) to walk along the left bank, with wonderful views of Burrator reservoir to the left. Follow the leat on; there are various crossing places and you should cross back to the right bank before descending to the valley of the **Meavy**; the leat picks up speed as it rushes downhill here, and the path is steep and rocky.

⑤ The **Meavy** is crossed via an aqueduct and the leat turns left. Take the grassy path right leading slightly uphill away from the river (there is a wealth of tin working evidence in the valley – worth an exploration). The path passes through a tumbledown granite wall; turn left and climb steeply up to **Black Tor**.

⑥ Go straight on past the **Logan Stone**, one of several on Dartmoor balanced in such a way that they can be rocked on their base, and on across open moorland to the road, with views of Brentor, Swelltor Quarries and the disused railway line ahead. Turn right at the road.

⑦ A few steps later, opposite the blocked off parking place, turn left and pick your way across tussocky grass, aiming for the mast on **North Hessary Tor**. This area is boggy in places, but passable.

⑧ At the railway track turn right and walk back to the edge of the town. The path splits, so keep left and through a small gate to join a tarmac road. Pass the **Devon Fire & Rescue Service** building to regain the car park on the right.

WHILE YOU'RE THERE   ⓘ

Visit the **High Moorland Visitor Centre** (open 10AM–5PM), situated in the old Duchy Hotel, which you pass on Point ①. You'll find everything you ever wanted to know about the Dartmoor National Park here, and more besides. There's an information centre and shop, helpful staff, and a range of audio-visual and 'hands-on' displays.

Walk 3

Around Lustleigh Cleave

A hard – yet rewarding – exploration of the wooded Bovey Valley.

•DISTANCE•	5 miles (8km)
•MINIMUM TIME•	3hrs
•ASCENT / GRADIENT•	754ft (230m) ▲▲ ▲
•LEVEL OF DIFFICULTY•	
•PATHS•	Steep rocky ascents/descents, rough paths and woodland
•LANDSCAPE•	Deeply wooded river valley and open moorland
•SUGGESTED MAP•	aqua3 OS Explorer OL28 Dartmoor
•START / FINISH•	Grid reference: SX 774815
•DOG FRIENDLINESS•	Dogs can run free but take care with livestock
•PARKING•	By side of lane at Hammerslake
•PUBLIC TOILETS•	Kes Tor Inn at Water

BACKGROUND TO THE WALK

Lustleigh is one of those perfect Devon villages that everyone just has to see. The rose-covered cottages and pub cluster tightly around the green and 13th-century Church of St John the Baptist. The quintessentially English cricket field, rushing streams and boulder-strewn hillslopes, all nestling together in a deep wooded valley beneath the eastern fringe of Dartmoor, make this a real magnet. But Lustleigh has a problem (or perhaps an advantage?) – there is no car park, meaning that many people weave their way through the cars parked around the church and drive off again in frustration. But there is another way of getting a feel for the real Lustleigh: drive on through the village, park, and walk back in.

On a Clear Day…

From the ridge approaching Hunter's Tor (after Point ②) you get a superb 360-degree view. To the south you can see the coast at Teignmouth. Following around clockwise you can pick out the familiar outline of Haytor, then Hound Tor (resembling a pack of hounds frozen in flight), Hayne Down and Bowerman's Nose, Manaton church and rocks, Easdon Tor, North Bovey, the Manor House Hotel, then Moretonhampstead with Mardon Down behind. Continuing round there is the stark outline of Blackingstone Rock then, far beyond on the Haldon Hills, the white tower of Haldon Belvedere, a folly erected in 1770 by Sir Robert Palk in memory of Major General Stringer Lawrence, the 'father of the Indian army'.

Lustleigh still holds a traditional May Day ceremony, which takes place on the first Saturday in May. The festival had died out, but was revived in the early years of the 20th century by Cecil Torr who, while living at Wreyland, wrote his famous three-volume work *Small Talk at Wreyland*, a charming record of rural life. The crowning ceremony at that time took place at Long Tor on the outskirts of the village. The May Queen, dressed in white and garlanded with spring flowers (and elected from the local children – candidates must have danced around the maypole on at least five previous occasions) leads a procession around the village beneath a canopy of flowers which is held aloft by other Lustleigh children. She is then crowned on the May Day rock in the Town Orchard. A new granite throne was set in place on the rock to celebrate the Millennium, and the names of recent May Queens are carved below.

Walk 3

Walk 3 Directions

① With **Lustleigh** village behind you, walk straight ahead from your car and turn left up a narrow rocky path between the houses **Loganstones** and **Grove**, following bridleway signs '**Cleave for Water**'. At the gate go straight ahead signed '**Hunter's Tor**' and climb steeply up to the top, where there are wide views over the moor.

② Turn right through oak woodland; the vegetation clears, and you follow the path straight on over the highest part of the ridge (1,063ft/324m) and across the remains of the Iron-Age fort to reach **Hunter's Tor**.

③ Pass through the gate to the right of the tor and follow the signed path right to meet another signed path left. Follow the track downhill through one gate, then immediately right through another and downhill towards **Peck Farm**. Go through the gate and straight on down the concrete drive.

④ Shortly after, turn left through a gate signed '**Foxworthy Bridge**' and continue along a wooded track. Pass through two gates to reach the beautiful thatched hamlet at **Foxworthy**; turn right.

⑤ Almost immediately go left, signed '**Horsham**'. Follow the track into mixed woodland through a gate. After 5 minutes or so follow signs right for '**Horsham for Manaton & Water**', to reach the **River Bovey**. Follow the riverbank left for a few paces to the crossing (on boulders) at **Horsham Steps**. Note: If you are concerned about crossing the river at Horsham Steps,

don't turn left for 'Horsham' at Point ⑤, go right down the drive, which crosses the river. Take the first footpath left and follow the river until you rejoin the main route at Point ⑥.

⑥ Cross over, taking care, to enter a nature reserve. Follow the path steeply uphill through woodland and over a stile. Keep left at two junctions then pass through a gate by two pretty cottages (note the tree-branch porch) following signs for 'Water' through **Letchole Plantation**.

⑦ At the crossroads of tracks turn right ('**Manaton direct**') to meet the lane by cottages at **Water**. Take the second lane right to the **Kes Tor Inn**.

⑧ Retrace your steps to the crossroads. Go straight on downhill to a split in the track. Keep left through a gate and continue down the steep, stony path (signed '**Clam Bridge for Lustleigh Cleave**'). Cross the river on the split-log bridge and proceed steeply uphill to the signpost left, '**Lustleigh via Hammerslake**'. Go left and left again at the next signpost (very steep). Pass a large granite boulder and follow the signs for **Hammerslake**. At the gate turn right down the rocky path back to the lane at the start.

WHERE TO EAT AND DRINK ⓘ

The **Kes Tor Inn** at Water has a range of bar snacks. On summer afternoons cream teas are often served at **Manaton village hall**, near the church. The thatched 15th-century **Cleave Inn** at Lustleigh has a delightful garden and serves excellent food. The **Primrose Cottage Tearooms** provide the perfect setting for a Devon cream tea.

A Look at Lustleigh Village

A less taxing way through Lustleigh Cleave – and a return through Wreyland.
See map and information panel for Walk 3

Walk 4

•DISTANCE•	4 miles (6.4km)
•MINIMUM TIME•	2hrs
•ASCENT / GRADIENT•	460ft (140m) ▲▲▲
•LEVEL OF DIFFICULTY•	

Walk 4 Directions (Walk 3 option)

If you'd prefer a slightly easier alternative to Walk 18, and want to see the village itself, this will suit you better, but it's still quite tough.

Walk back along the lane towards **Lustleigh**. Pass **Waye Farm** and, shortly after, turn right up a stony track signed 'Lustleigh Cleave', Point Ⓐ. Pass through **Heaven's Gate** and proceed downhill into the valley. Turn left into Woodland Trust land. Follow grassy paths to a track at the bottom of the hill.

Turn left through conifers, past the ivy-covered ruins of **Boveycombe Farm**, to reach a fork. Go right towards the old packhorse bridge at **Hisley**, Point Ⓑ. Don't cross over; turn left and follow the river over a stile into the **Bovey Valley Woodlands**. Cross a second stile along the riverbank, pass through a gate and across the field to join a lane at a metal gate.

Turn left uphill and take the first lane right. Soon take the footpath signed 'Wreyland' right, Point Ⓒ. Follow the path to cross the bridge over **Wray Brook**. Go left (note the old railway viaduct on the left) and follow the signs along the field edge then through a gate into **Wreyland**.

Turn left to pass **Wreyland Manor** (dating from the 1360s, but altered in 1680) and cricket pitch and enter **Lustleigh** by the green, the oldest part, with its stone cross erected in memory of Henry Tudor, rector 1888–1904. Turn left at the church and go straight ahead between the dairy and post office into the **Town Orchard**. Carry on past the May Day rock to the end of the orchard and cross the leat on a wooden bridge. Go through the gate and, at the next junction of paths, drop down right to see the magical granite 'footbridge'.

Retrace your steps to the junction and go straight over to join the lane. Turn left, then first right to zig-zag very steeply up a lane to **Pethybridge**, between two thatched cottages. Turn left, then right at the top. Walk past **Waye Farm** and return to your car.

WHILE YOU'RE THERE ⓘ
Becka Falls are just south of Manaton on the Bovey Tracey road. This natural waterfall, where the Becka Brook tumbles more than 80ft (24m) over a succession of huge granite boulders, is at its most impressive after heavy rainfall.

Walk 5

The Terrifying Sea Along the Coast to Start Point

The sea has left a sobering reminder of its strength on the coast from Slapton Ley to Start Point.

•DISTANCE•	6 miles (9.7km)
•MINIMUM TIME•	3hrs
•ASCENT / GRADIENT•	328ft (100m) ▲▲▲
•LEVEL OF DIFFICULTY•	
•PATHS•	Good coast path, 1 stile
•LANDSCAPE•	Undulating cliffs and shingle beaches
•SUGGESTED MAP•	aqua3 OS Explorer OL20 South Devon
•START / FINISH•	Grid reference: SX 823420
•DOG FRIENDLINESS•	Dogs to be kept under control at all times
•PARKING•	Long stay car park at Torcross
•PUBLIC TOILETS•	In Torcross and by beach at North Hallsands

Walk 5 Directions

Visit the little village of Torcross, at the southern end of Slapton Ley, south of Dartmouth, on a sunny summer's day and it's quite impossible to believe that it could ever be anything but warm, calm and tranquil. The views south to Start Point are particularly wonderful in May, when the point shimmers under a carpet of bluebells. But on 16 January 1917 the fishing village of Hallsands, just to the south, was almost totally destroyed during a huge storm which smashed through the sea walls and washed the cottages away. Perhaps it was the result of extensive dredging work off the coast here between 1897 and 1902, when tons of shingle were removed for Royal Navy building work at Devonport in Plymouth. Around 1,600 tons were dredged up each day, so altering the patterns of coastal erosion. The remaining

villages still suffer – Torcross sea front was badly damaged during heavy storms in 1951 and 1979.

This is a versatile walk, giving a good feel for the coastline. You can turn back at **Beesands**, or **Hallsands**, or go all the way to the lighthouse at **Start Point**. From the blocked-off path to ruined Hallsands village, you can still see the remains of some of the cottages.

> ### WHAT TO LOOK FOR ⓘ
> You'll notice an American **Sherman tank** in the car park, which was lost during the D-Day landing practices in 1944, and recovered from the sea in 1984. It now stands as a memorial to those American servicemen who perished during Operation Tiger, a training exercise that went tragically wrong in the early hours of 28 April 1944. Nine German torpedo boats intercepted a 3-mile (4.8km) long convoy of US vessels moving from Portland to Slapton Sands during a landing rehearsal. Two landing craft were destroyed, and two more damaged, leading to the loss of almost 1,000 lives.

Walk 5

WHERE TO EAT AND DRINK ℹ️

The **Start Bay Inn**, opposite the car park, is a free house and welcomes families, and there's fish and chips at Torcross too. The **Cricket Inn**, at tucked-away Beesands, has a great atmosphere, and specialises in seafood. It serves traditional ales, and has a little beer garden, but the best place to sit and relax is on the sea wall. There's a lovely garden too at **Trout's**, just above the remains of Hallsands village, where you can enjoy tea or excellent local ice cream en route for Start Point. There's also a seasonal **beach café** at North Hallsands.

You glimpse the ruins from various points along the coast path, too.

Follow the footpath sign over the road to turn right along the concrete **promenade** (a sea defence scheme from 1980). At the end ascend steep steps on to a gritty track, following coast path signs, with great views back along **Slapton Ley**. This, the largest natural lake in the West Country, is a haven for goldeneye, grey herons, mute swans, tufted ducks, pochards, great crested grebes, mallards, moorhens and coots, and is popular with birdwatchers. There's a good information board by the **Duckery** near the car park.

Go through a gate into a field on the cliff top, then through the next gate and along a track which drops down with spectacular views over Widdicombe Ley and Beesands. The track runs behind the beach into the village, which has a slightly forgotten feel about it. Pass the tiny **St Andrew's Church** and the **Cricket Inn** (on the right), and continue straight on, following signs for Hallsands. Follow the path as it climbs steeply up the cliff and on through a brackeny area. When

North Hallsands comes into view, look carefully down to sea level to the ruined village beyond.

Go through the next gate and along the lower edge of the field. The beach at **North Hallsands** is quiet and remote, the houses across the field behind the beach were built to re-house some of the displaced villagers in 1924. Another gate leads into the next field; go through the next gate and field to reach the beach. Cross the beach to join the lane leading to **Hallsands Hotel**, then follow the coast path '**Start Point**' up steps behind the hotel. This leads on to Trout's holiday apartments above Hallsands, former home to the indomitable Trout sisters, survivors of the devastation of 1917. Walk down to the gate above the old path to the village and look down at the ruins; there's a real feeling of desolation here.

Continue to follow the coast path towards **Start Point**. A couple of old apple trees have been blown over the path to form arches, giving an idea of the strength of the winds here. The path leads up to a stile to join the car park for **Start Point** and **Great Mattisombe Sand**, and the gate to the lighthouse. There are spectacular views back to South Hallsands and all along the length of the coast.

Down, Ditch and Dyke from Pentridge

A stiff climb leads to a dramatic defensive earthwork.

•DISTANCE•	3½ miles (5.7km)
•MINIMUM TIME•	2hrs
•ASCENT / GRADIENT•	475ft (145m) ▲▲▲
•LEVEL OF DIFFICULTY•	
•PATHS•	Steep, muddy farmland, grassy sward, farm roads, 4 stiles
•LANDSCAPE•	Chalk downs, open grassland, fields and copse
•SUGGESTED MAP•	aqua3 OS Explorer 118 Shaftesbury & Cranborne Chase
•START / FINISH•	Grid reference: SU 034178
•DOG FRIENDLINESS•	No problems
•PARKING•	Lay-by in Pentridge or start from car park at Martin Down
•PUBLIC TOILETS•	None on route

BACKGROUND TO THE WALK

At 607ft (185m) high, Penbury Knoll has made a good lookout over Cranborne Chase since settlers first left their mark on this quiet corner of north east Dorset, some 5,000 years ago. The maps show signs of Celtic field systems (associated with the period around 1000 BC) plotted around the lovely green combe of Pentridge Down, though little is revealed to the naked eye. The extraordinary Dorset Cursus starts to the north of here and the landscape is littered with lumpy burial mounds, or tumuli, and long barrows, the most visible signs of early settlement. Grim's Ditch marked a Bronze-Age farm boundary, but a more significant defensive earthwork remains from this period, constructed to protect the long-vanished hill fort against invasion from the north east.

Bokerley Dyke

Bokerley Dyke is a broad scar running down the hill. It consists of a high bank and deep ditch, which originally extended for some 3 miles (4.8km). A matter of a weeks' work for a JCB, the construction of the dyke must have taken thousands of hours of punishing hard labour. In the 4th century AD it was strengthened and parts of it were re-dug, as by then it formed an important defence on the Roman route along Ackling Dyke to the stronghold at Badbury Rings, against Saxon invaders. In the 9th century it again formed a vital part of the defence of Dorset – this time from attacks by the Vikings, who were overrunning the Kingdom of Wessex. King Ethelred I was mortally wounded in a fierce battle on Martin Down, on the other side of the dyke, in AD 871. This event left the way open for his younger brother Alfred to claim the throne of Wessex and eventually make a successful peace with the marauding Danes.

Pentridge

There has been a settlement below the hill at Pentridge since at least the recordings of the Domesday survey in the 11th century, when St Rumbold's Church received its first mention. The quiet hamlet of Pentridge is spared the modern invasion of traffic passing through.

Tiled cob walls mix with flint and brick and thatch, and there's a handsome 18th-century barn. Unusually, little Chestnut Cottage, by the turning to the church, has exposed timbers. Unlike busier villages, where houses jostle forward on to the narrow pavements, here they are set back from the single main street, tucked behind hedges and gardens, or in a silent line further up the hill. There's no orange streetlighting here. In the dusk, little squares of golden light appear, unshaded by curtains, evoking memories of Thomas Hardy's obsession in *The Woodlanders* (1887) with lamps and firelight and looking through people's windows to see life played out.

Walk 6

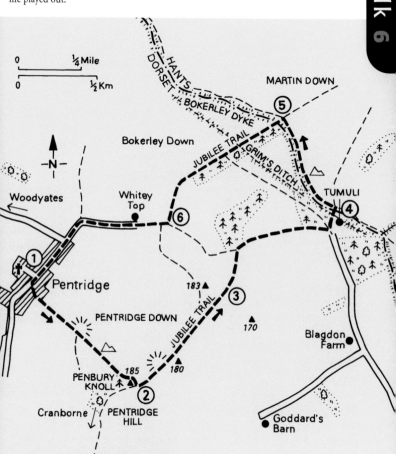

Walk 6 Directions

① From the lay-by walk past the turning up to the church and cross the stile on the left by the footpath sign. Head up the field to a stile, and cross it to enter a narrow footpath. This leads between hedges, straight up the 610ft

(185m) **Pentridge Hill**. Cross another stile into a field and keep straight ahead. As you pause to catch your breath, you can start to admire the view opening around you, with the green curve of Pentridge Down on the left. Keep straight on to the top of the hill (**Penbury Knoll**), passing to the left of a clump of trees.

Walk 6

② At the top turn left on to the **Jubilee Trail** footpath, which runs along the ridge of the down beside an ancient hedge line. (There are fabulous views on either side – Pentridge is largely hidden in the trees.) After ½ mile (800m) the path starts to descend.

WHILE YOU'RE THERE ⓘ
Explore **Martin Down**, on the other side of the dyke, and just over the border into Hampshire. A National Nature Reserve in the care of English Nature, it consists of open tracts of chalk downland, dotted with wild flowers including purple clover, lilac-coloured scabious and soft blue harebells, with heath, scrub and woodland.

③ Turn right, through a gate into a copse, following the Jubilee Trail marker, and descend along the field edge. Soon bear left across the field to a fingerpost in the hedge, to turn right down a muddy track. There are good views of Bokerley Dyke curving away to your left. Descend through woodland to a gate at the bottom. Go through and turn right, on to a bridleway. Pass a metal gate and immediately hook back left on a chalky track. As you start to descend, curious mounds appear to the right – tumuli.

④ Cross **Grim's Ditch** and **Bokerley Dyke** on to the nature reserve of **Martin Down**, and immediately turn left on to the grassy path, which runs along the east side of the ditch. Follow this

WHAT TO LOOK FOR ⓘ
St Rumbold's Church was rebuilt in 1855 and is a pleasing, unfussy structure of grey stone and flint. Look out for a plaque inside commemorating one Robert Browning who died in 1746: he was a butler and the great-great-grandfather of the famous Victorian poet of the same name.

downhill for ½ mile (800m).

⑤ At the crossroads of tracks turn left on to the **Jubilee Trail**, by the fingerpost that announces it's only 90 miles (144km) to Forde Abbey. A nettly path runs up the side of mixed woodland. At the end of the woods go straight ahead, through a gate. Follow the field boundary up to the top and cross the stile.

⑥ Turn right and go through the farm gate into a green lane. **Pentridge Down** emerges to the left, with the village hidden by trees. Pass through another gate on to a farm track between high hedges. Continue down to the bottom and follow it round to the left. Walk back into the village along the main

Uley and its Magnificent Fort on the Hill

The vast bulk of the ancient fort of Uley Bury forms the centrepiece for this walk along the Cotswold escarpment.

Walk 7

•DISTANCE•	3 miles (4.8km)
•MINIMUM TIME•	1hr 30min
•ASCENT / GRADIENT•	345ft (105m) ▲▲▲
•LEVEL OF DIFFICULTY•	
•PATHS•	Tracks and fields
•LANDSCAPE•	Valley, meadows, woodland and open hilltop
•SUGGESTED MAP•	aqua3 OS Explorer 168 Stroud, Tetbury and Malmesbury
•START / FINISH•	Grid reference: ST 789984
•DOG FRIENDLINESS•	Good – little or no livestock, few stiles
•PARKING•	Main street of Uley
•PUBLIC TOILETS•	None on route

BACKGROUND TO THE WALK

Uley is a pretty village, strung along a wide street at the foot of a high, steep hill. It is distinctive for several reasons. It has its own brewery, which produces some fine beers including Uley Bitter and Uley Old Spot. In the past the village specialised in the production of 'Uley Blue' cloth, which was used in military uniforms. And then there is Uley Bury, dating back to the Iron Age and one of the finest hill forts in the Cotswolds.

Peaceful Settlements

There are many hundreds of Iron-Age forts throughout England and Wales. They are concentrated in Cornwall, south west Wales and the Welsh Marches, with secondary concentrations throughout the Cotswolds, North Wales, Wessex and the north of England. Although the term 'hill fort' is generally used in connection with these settlements, the term can be misleading. There are many that were built on level ground and there are many that were not used purely for military purposes – often they were simply settlements located on easily defended sites. Broadly speaking, there are five types, classified according to the nature of the site on which they were built, rather than, say, the date of their construction. Contour forts were built more or less along the perimeter edge of a hilltop; promontory forts were built on a spur, surrounded by natural defences on two or more sides; valley and plateau forts (two types) depended heavily on artificial defences and were located, as their names suggest, in valleys or on flat land respectively; and multiple-enclosure forts were usually built in a poor strategic position on the slope of a hill and were perhaps used as stockades for protecting cattle.

Natural Defences

Uley Bury, covering about 38 acres (15.4ha), is classified as an inland promontory fort and was built in the 6th century BC. It falls away on three sides, the fourth side, which faces away from the escarpment, is protected by specially constructed ramparts which would have been surmounted by a wooden palisade. The natural defences – that is, the Cotswold escarpment, facing west – were also strengthened by the construction of a wide and deep ditch, as well as two additional ramparts, an inner one and an outer one, between which the footpath largely threads its course. The three main entrances were at the northern, eastern and southern corners. These, being the most vulnerable parts of the fort, would have been fortified with massive log barriers.

Although some tribespeople would have lived permanently in huts within the fort, most would have lived outside, either on other parts of the hill or in the valleys below. In an emergency, therefore, there was space for those who lived outside the fort to take shelter within. Eventually the fort was taken over by the Dobunni tribe – Celtic interlopers from mainland Europe who arrived about 100 BC – and appears to have been occupied by them throughout the Roman era.

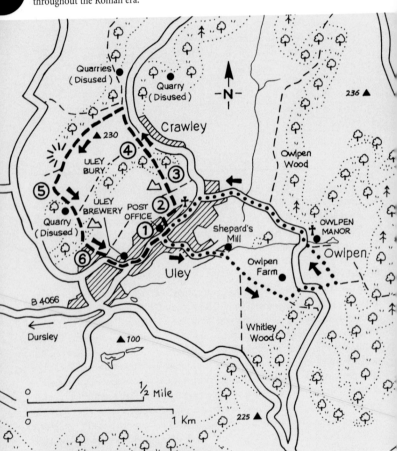

Walk 7 **Directions**

① From the main street locate the **post office** (on your left as you walk up the street). Walk along the narrow lane (to the right, as you look at it). Pass between houses as the lane dwindles to a track. Immediately before a stile turn right along an enclosed path towards the **church**.

Walk 7

② When the churchyard can be seen on the right, turn left up a narrow path beside a cottage. This rises fairly sharply and brings you to a kissing gate. Pass through into a meadow. Climb steeply up the grassland towards woodland.

③ At the treeline keep left of the woods. In a corner go through a gate and follow a winding woodland path, climbing among the trees. When you come to a fence stay on the path as it bears left. Go over a stile and then continue ascending, to emerge from the woods. Stay on the path as it rises across grassland to a junction.

WHAT TO LOOK FOR ℹ
There are **magnificent views** westward from the summit of Uley Bury. You should easily be able to see the estuary of the River Severn, as well as the Tyndale Monument. Look out too for the **brewery** in Uley and the statue of a pig outside it. This is a Gloucester Old Spot, a breed of pig peculiar to the county, now making something of a comeback.

④ Turn right to follow the contour of the hill – the edge of the ancient fort. You are following the perimeter of the fort in an anti-clockwise direction, with steep drops to your right. When you meet another junction of paths go left along the edge of the hill, with views to the west.

⑤ At the next corner continue to follow the edge of the fort, disregarding a stile that invites you to descend. At the next corner, at the fort's south eastern point, bear right on a path that descends through hillocks and then quite steeply through bushes, keeping left. This will bring you to a stile into a meadow and a tarmac path.

WHERE TO EAT AND DRINK ℹ
The **Old Crown** on the main street opposite the church in Uley is a very picturesque village local, with lots of memorabilia on the walls, exposed beams and a small, sunny garden. Beers come from the local brewery and include Uley Bitter and Uley Old Spot, named after the Gloucestershire pigs.

⑥ Walk along the path, all the way to a cottage and then a kissing gate. Go through this and pass beside the cottage to arrive at a lane. Turn left here and follow the lane, soon passing the **Uley Brewery**, to reach the main road. Turn left, passing **South Street**, to return to the start.

Extending the Walk
While you're in Uley you can make an interesting additional circuit by walking up **South Street** from the main street. Cross fields to the right of **Owlpen Farm** then pick out a route into **Owlpen** village with its ancient **manor house**. You can return to Uley on the road.

WHILE YOU'RE THERE ℹ
Two sites are worth a closer look while you're in the area. Near by is the little village of North Nibley, over which towers the 111ft (34m) **Tyndale Monument**. Built in 1866 this is a tribute to William Tyndale (c1494–1536). He was born at Dursley near Gloucester, and was the first to translate the New Testament of the Bible from Latin into English. It is possible to climb to near the top of the tower for magnificent views. Just to the north of Uley Bury, and still on the escarpment, is Uley Long Barrow, better known as **Hetty Pegler's Tump**. This is a neolithic chambered tomb some 180ft (55m) in length. A narrow stone doorway leads into a passage, off which four semicircular chambers would have contained cremated remains.

Walk 8

Horner's Corners

On the trail of Exmoor's red deer in the woodlands under Dunkery Beacon.

•DISTANCE•	4½ miles (7.2km)
•MINIMUM TIME•	2hrs 30min
•ASCENT / GRADIENT•	1,000ft (300m) ▲▲▲
•LEVEL OF DIFFICULTY•	
•PATHS•	Broad paths, with some stonier ones, steep in places, no stiles
•LANDSCAPE•	Dense woodland in steep-sided stream valleys
•SUGGESTED MAP•	aqua3 OS Explorer OL9 Exmoor
•START / FINISH•	Grid reference: SS 898455
•DOG FRIENDLINESS•	Off lead, but be aware of deer and horse-riders
•PARKING•	National Trust car park (free) at Horner
•PUBLIC TOILETS•	At car park

BACKGROUND TO THE WALK

Horner takes its name from the Saxon 'hwrnwr', a wonderfully expressive word meaning snorer, that here describes the rumble of the stream in its enclosed valley. Above the treetops, Webber's Post is a splendid viewpoint out across the Bristol Channel. What Mr Webber stood there to view, though, was the hunting of red deer.

The herd on Exmoor numbers several thousand. Although this is small compared to those in the Scottish Highlands, the Exmoor stag himself is the UK's biggest wild deer. This is simply because his life is slightly easier – farmed deer are larger again. On Exmoor, as in the rest of Northern Europe outside Scotland, the deer remains a forest animal. Exmoor's mix of impenetrable woodland with areas of open grazing, even with all its houses, farms and fields, remains good deer country.

The calf is born dappled for camouflage under the trees, and lies in shelter during the day while the hind feeds. If you do come across a deer calf, leave it alone – it hasn't been abandoned. During the summer the stags and hinds run in separate herds. In the Scottish Highlands deer graze on high ground during the day to escape from midges, and descend to the forest at night; on Exmoor the main annoying pest is the human, so the deer graze the moor at dawn and dusk, and spend the day in the trees.

Stag Nights

In September and October comes the spectacular rut, when stags roar defiance at each other, and, if that fails, do battle with antlers for mating privileges. During this time they eat only occasionally, fight a lot and mate as often as possible. The stag with a mighty roar and a hard head can gather a harem of a dozen hinds. Your best chance of seeing one is very early or very late in the day – or else in the forest. I have had a bramble patch beside my path suddenly start bouncing around like an angry saucepan of milk, until, after ten seconds, a half-grown calf burst out of the middle of it and ran away. You may well smell the deer, even though it probably smelled you first and has already gone quietly away. Look closely, too, at the small brown cows two fields away – they may well be deer. I've seen grazing deer from a train window just five minutes out of Taunton Station, though they were the smaller roe.

While deer are thriving, it's the Exmoor stag hunters that are in danger of extinction. Just one pack of the traditional staghounds remains. Following pressure from its own members, the National Trust has banned hunting from its land, and the national government is set to ban it altogether when it finds the parliamentary time.

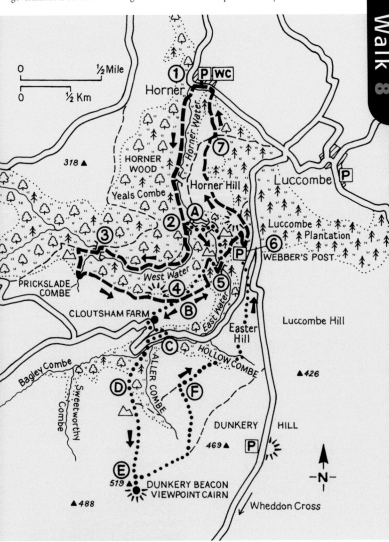

Walk 8 **Directions**

① Leave the National Trust car park in Horner village past the toilets and turn right to the track leading into **Horner Wood**. This crosses a bridge and passes a field before rejoining **Horner Water**. You can take a footpath alongside the stream instead of the track, they lead to the same place. Ignore the first footbridge, and continue along the obvious track to where a sign, '**Dunkery Beacon**', points off to the left towards a second footbridge.

Walk 8

② Ignore this footbridge as well (unless you're on Walk 9). Keep on the track for another 100yds (91m), then fork left on a path alongside **West Water**. This rejoins the track, and after another ½ mile (800m) a bridleway sign points back to the right. Here look down to the left for a footbridge. For me this was a thrilling balancing act on two girders – but the rebuilding of the bridge (swept away in floods in 2001) has now been completed.

③ Cross on to a path that slants up to the right. After 200yds (183m) turn left into a smaller path that turns uphill alongside **Prickslade Combe**. The path reaches the combe's little stream at a cross-path, with the wood top visible above. Here turn left, across the stream, on a path contouring through the top of the wood. It emerges into the open and arrives at a tree with a bench and a fine view over the top of the woodlands to Porlock Bay.

④ Continue ahead on a grassy track, with the car park of Webber's Post clearly visible ahead. Alas, the

deep valley of the East Water lies between you and your destination. So, turn down left on a clear path back into birchwoods. This zig-zags down to meet a larger track in the valley bottom.

⑤ Turn downstream, crossing a footbridge over the **East Water**, beside a ford. After about 60yds (55m) bear right on to an ascending path. At the top of the steep section turn right on a small sunken path that climbs gently to **Webber's Post** car park.

⑥ Walk to the left, round the car park, to a path marked 'Permitted Bridleway' to **Horner**. (Do not take the pink-surfaced, easy-access path immediately to the right.) After 80yds (73m) bear left on to a wider footpath. Keep ahead down a wide, gentle spur, with the deep valley of the **Horner Water** on your left. As the spur steepens, the footpath meets a crossing track signposted 'Windsor Path'.

⑦ Turn right for perhaps 30 paces, then take a descending path signposted '**Horner**'. Narrow at first, this widens and finally meets a wide, horse-mangled track with wooden steps; turn left down this

Fire at Dunkery Beacon

A moorland extension leads up to the high point of Somerset.
See map and information panel for Walk 8

•**DISTANCE**•	6 miles (9.7km)
•**MINIMUM TIME**•	3hrs 40min
•**ASCENT / GRADIENT**•	1,700ft (520m) ▲ ▲ ▲
•**LEVEL OF DIFFICULTY**•	
•**PATHS**•	Rough paths in Horner Woods, stony hill descent, 2 stiles

Walk 9 Directions
(Walk 8 option)

At Point ② of Walk 8, Point Ⓐ, turn left over the bridge, signposted 'Dunkery Beacon'. A wide path leads up **East Water**, crossing to its left side by ford and footbridge. After ¼ mile (400m) it crosses back, and very shortly a path branches off on the right. It climbs in zig-zags, and then more gently, to a cross-track and bench, Point Ⓑ, (also Point ④ on Walk 8). Cross the path and ascend to a gate. Follow the left edge of a field to another gate and stile, to a track to **Cloutsham Farm**. Turn left past the buildings and, where the road bends, descend a track to rejoin the road lower down, Point Ⓒ.

Turn up the road, past a picnic field. Just after a bridge on the left a stream runs down to join the **East Water** and, a few steps further on, a wide path sets off across the stream, up the wooded spur and on to the open hill, Point Ⓓ.

After 120yds (110m) a contouring path crosses your own: this is **Dicky's Path**. To bypass Dunkery Hill simply turn left here to pass through the woods of **Aller Combe** and continue from Point Ⓕ; otherwise follow the clear path uphill. As the slope eases a wider, stony path joins from the left – this will be your descent route. The huge cairn is just beyond, Point Ⓔ.

Near by is a viewpoint cairn, with a topograph. Follow the ascent route back for 110yds (100m) and bear right on the wider, stony path. This runs down to the tip of **Aller Combe**, now a mere groove in the heather. After another 25yds (23m) turn down left on a smaller path. After 600yds (549m) it passes three hawthorns and shortly a fourth one marks the junction with Dicky's Path, Point Ⓕ.

Turn right on **Dicky's Path**, contouring through heather and thorn. It runs in and out of the steeply wooded **Hollow Combe**, where the path is protected with a handrail. Walk softly, for here you might see red deer.(Some say that if you smile and wave the deer will consider you a harmless idiot and allow you to approach more closely, but it's never worked for me.) When you emerge on to open ground fork left on a smaller path, through gorse and heather, to **Webber's Post** car park, Point ⑥.

Walk 10

Sarsen Stones on Fyfield Down

Explore a prehistoric landscape on this fascinating downland ramble.

•DISTANCE•	6 miles (9.7km)
•MINIMUM TIME•	2hrs 30min
•ASCENT / GRADIENT•	328ft (100m) ▲ ▲ ▲
•LEVEL OF DIFFICULTY•	
•PATHS•	Downland tracks and field paths
•LANDSCAPE•	Lofty downland pasture and gallops
•SUGGESTED MAP•	aqua3 OS Explorer 157 Marlborough & Savernake Forest
•START / FINISH•	Grid reference: SU 159699
•DOG FRIENDLINESS•	Can be off lead along Ridgeway path
•PARKING•	Car park close to Manton House Estate (right off A4, signed Manton, west of Marlborough)
•PUBLIC TOILETS•	None on route

Walk 10 Directions

Leave the car park by the track in the top right-hand corner, signposted '**White Horse Trail to Avebury and Hackpen**'. Follow the track right and shortly fork left, continuing between high hedges (private roads right), then on between the gallops across **Clatford Down** with good views. On reaching a T-junction by a covered reservoir, turn left along the **Herepath** (Green Street).

The Herepath is an ancient east–west route across the Marlborough Downs. The name is

WHERE TO EAT AND DRINK ⓘ

There are no refreshment places along the route but, if you bring your own, the Ridgeway track with its far-reaching views provides the perfect picnic spot. Nearby Manton and Lockeridge have pubs, while Marlborough offers the full range of refreshment facilities.

derived from the Old English word 'here' meaning an army or multitude. It suggests that this may have been one of the defensive routes established by King Alfred in the 9th century in his struggle with the Danes.

Shortly, turn right through a gate waymarked '**Hackpen**', to join a grassy track alongside a conifer plantation, then head across pasture to a gate into woodland. Follow the track (can be muddy) through the sparse woodland then, on leaving the wood, keep straight on along the right-hand field edge. Turn left down a track in the field corner. Pass a gate on the right and continue between fields to reach the **Ridgeway**. This ancient highway incorporates a complicated network of green lanes, and follows a natural route on high ground. It was used as a drove road or trading route and a convenient means for invaders, peaceful or war-like, to penetrate the heartland of southern England before Anglo-Saxon times. The Ridgeway National Trail forms only part of the route, although by linking several trails you can walk the entire length.

Turn left along the rutted and often muddy track for ¾ mile (1.2km) then, at the crossways by an information board, turn left through a gate on to **Fyfield Down**.

A feature of Fyfield Down and neighbouring Overton Down are the sarsen stones that litter this intriguing chalk limestone landscape. Sarsens are natural deposits of extremely hard siliceous sandstone that derive from Tertiary deposits, later eroded and moved by glaciation some 25 million years ago. Although found elsewhere, they are not on the scale seen in the Marlborough district. Sarsens are also known as 'druid stones' or 'grey wethers', the latter due to their resemblance at a distance to a flock of sheep, the word 'wether' coming from the Old English for sheep.

Sarsens have been of great importance to humans since prehistoric times. The hard flints were used to make hand axes and other useful tools during the Bronze Age. From the 5th century to the mid-19th century, sarsens were used for building stone, constructing the nearby villages of West Overton and Lockeridge, gateposts, and as paving stones and tramway setts. More importantly, Fyfield Down was the stone quarry supplying Avebury stone circle and possibly Stonehenge. Stones weighing as much as 40 tons were dug up, sometimes shaped, and dragged over the downs by hundreds of people pulling them on wooden rollers with woven grass ropes.

In 1956 Fyfield Down was declared a National Nature Reserve, not only to protect this fine stretch of natural downland and Britain's best assemblage of sarsen stones, which support nationally important lichens, but also to preserve the extensive prehistoric field systems that exist here. As you stride across this rock-strewn landscape, note the chequerboard appearance of the field systems. Banks or 'lynchets' some 8ft (3m) high have formed where sarsens had been moved to create field boundaries, arresting soil movement caused by ploughing over the centuries.

> **WHILE YOU'RE THERE**
> Visit **Avebury** to view the largest stone circle in Europe and explore the fascinating Alexander Keiller Museum to learn more about the prehistoric archaeology of this area.

Proceed along a grassy track and cross a **gallop** via three gates. This is prime racehorse training country and there are many racing stables in the area. Continue to the right of a wood then, in the valley bottom, fork right off the gravel track and ascend a grassy track, passing more sarsen stones. At the top, go through the two gates that cut the corner of a wooded enclosure and turn right along the field edge, ignoring the stile on the right. Pass through a gate in the bottom corner, cross a gallop and continue straight on across grassland on a defined path. Cross another gallop, then follow the path right over a further gallop to a **furlong pole** at the end of a line of trees. Swing left over yet more gallops to a waymarker post, then turn left to cross two more gallops to reach a gate. Turn right and follow the outward route back to the car park.

Royal Romances at Polesden Lacey

A woodland circuit around a great country house that was once a favourite with high society.

•DISTANCE•	4¼ miles (6.8km)
•MINIMUM TIME•	2hrs 15min
•ASCENT / GRADIENT•	607ft (185m)
•LEVEL OF DIFFICULTY•	
•PATHS•	Woodland and farm tracks
•LANDSCAPE•	Remote wooded valleys around Polesden Lacey estate
•SUGGESTED MAP•	aqua3 OS Explorer 146 Dorking, Box Hill & Reigate
•START / FINISH•	Grid reference: TQ 141503
•DOG FRIENDLINESS•	The kind of walk that dogs dream about
•PARKING•	National Trust car park on Ranmore Common Road
•PUBLIC TOILETS•	Toilets at Polesden Lacey for visitors only

BACKGROUND TO THE WALK

To say that the history of Polesden Lacey is the history of the British monarchy through the early decades of the 20th century is, perhaps, overstating things. Nevertheless, in the years before World War Two the royal family's footfalls often echoed within these sumptuous walls.

Your Personal Tour

Even if you don't step beyond the Lacey's main gates, there's plenty of opportunity to see the house and grounds as you weave your way around the estate. Soon after the start of the walk, you'll get a stunning panorama across the terrace and formal lawns to the colonnaded south front, and you'll be glad of a pair of binoculars here. A little further on, you'll dive under the thatched bridge linking the formal gardens to the summer house and the old kitchen garden, and pass the entrance to the Home Farm. Then comes the main entrance at North Lodge, before you turn south and drop under the balustraded bridge that carries the drive from Chapel Lane.

Polesden Reborn

Late in the 18th century, the dramatist Richard Sheridan made his home at Polesden Lacey. Although he thought that it was 'the nicest place, within prudent distance of town, in England', the house was pulled down after his death. In 1823 a new Regency villa arose on the site, and this building now forms the core of the modern house. The Hon Ronald and Mrs Greville bought Polesden Lacey in 1906, extended and remodelled the house and its grounds, and set about transforming their new home into a focus of high society.

Royal Romances

The couple were not exactly without influence. King Edward VII was an intimate friend, and the cream of Edwardian aristocracy was drawn to Polesden Lacey by the stimulating company and Mrs Greville's impeccable hospitality. The royal family were frequent visitors through the inter-war years and the Duke and Duchess of York – later King George VI and Queen Elizabeth (the late Queen Mother) – came here for part of their honeymoon in 1923.

Ten years later, another royal romance ended in tears. The Prince of Wales was a particular favourite of Mrs Greville's but, by the mid-1930s, his liaison with the American divorcee Mrs Wallis Simpson was causing speculation on both sides of the Atlantic. When King George V died in 1936, and the new King declared his intention of marriage, it unleashed a constitutional storm that led to his abdication before the year's end.

Time was also running out for Polesden Lacey. Mrs Greville had just a few years left to live, and she bequeathed her home to the National Trust in 1942.

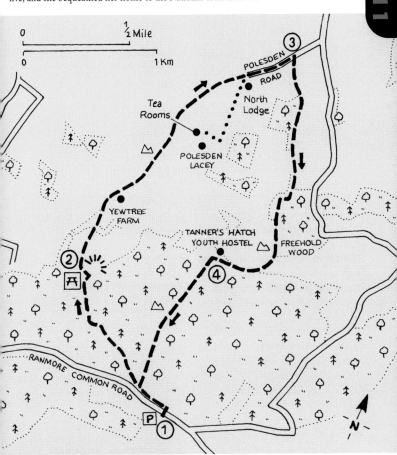

Walk 11 **Directions**

① Cross the road from the car park, turn left, and walk for 200yds (183m) along the broad roadside verge. Turn right just beyond the tile-hung **Fox Cottages**, where two public footpaths meet the road. Take the left-hand path through the woods and, ignoring all turnings, follow it through a little combe. At length it draws alongside a post and rail fence, and veers sharp left. Turn right here, through the gap in the fence, and continue through the

Walk 11

woodland glade. Just beyond a wooden gate, turn left on to the signposted **Yewtree Farm Walk**. Continue to the gravelled forest track 100yds (91m) further on, and turn right.

A little further on you'll come to a bench seat on your right. There's a great view of Polesden Lacey from here, and it's a good spot for a picnic. Notice the massive estate water tower sticking up through the trees, just to the left of the main house.

② Follow the gravelled track as it winds past **Yewtree Farm**; then, 150yds (137m) beyond the farm, fork left. Follow the signposted bridleway across a low causeway until it climbs to meet an estate road. Keep straight on, under a little thatched timber footbridge.

As you pass the entrance to **Home Farm House**, look half left across the open field. On the far horizon, you'll see a long, low white building – and, on a clear day, you'll be able to pick out the jets landing in front of it at Heathrow. Bear gently right

past the entrance drive to **Polesden Lacey**, and continue on to **Polesden Road**. Walk right to the end of the broad, grass verge on the right-hand side of the road; then, 60yds (55m) further on, turn right down a waymarked bridleway towards the youth hostel.

③ The track is relatively easy to follow. It zig-zags right and left into **Freehold Wood**, then dives under a stone-arched bridge. Continue down the sunken way, then bear right at the blue waymarker post at the bottom of the hill and climb up gently through the woods to **Tanner's Hatch**.

④ Bear left at the youth hostel and follow the yellow waymarked gravel track as it climbs up gently but steadily all the way back to **Ranmore Common Road**. Turn left for the last 200yds (183m) back to the car park.

Birling Gap to Beachy Head

A magnificent clifftop walk exploring a scenic stretch of the Sussex coast.

Walk 12

•DISTANCE•	7½ miles (12km)
•MINIMUM TIME•	3hrs
•ASCENT / GRADIENT•	536ft (163m) ▲▲▲
•LEVEL OF DIFFICULTY•	
•PATHS•	Downland paths and tracks, clifftop greensward, no stiles
•LANDSCAPE•	Southern boundary of South Downs and headland
•SUGGESTED MAP•	aqua3 OS Explorer 123 South Downs Way – Newhaven to Eastbourne
•START / FINISH•	Grid reference: TQ 554959
•DOG FRIENDLINESS•	On lead by Cornish Farm. Off lead on South Downs Way
•PARKING•	Free car park at Birling Gap
•PUBLIC TOILETS•	Birling Gap and Beachy Head

BACKGROUND TO THE WALK

The magnificent chalk cliffs of Beachy Head were formed from the shells of billions of minute creatures which fell to the bottom of a subtropical sea. Today, this stretch of coast is one of Britain's most famous landmarks. The treeless South Downs reach the sea in spectacular fashion and over 500ft (152m) below the towering cliffs lies Beachy Head's distinctive red and white lighthouse, standing alone on a remote beach. This blend of natural and artificial features creates a magnificent picture.

Devil's Cape

The present 142ft (43m) lighthouse, automated in 1983 and modernised in 1999, has been vital to the safety of mariners off this coast since it was completed in 1902. But even as far back as 1670 a beacon shone from this point, helping to guide ships away from the treacherous ledges below. Beachy Head has always been a navigational nightmare. Sailors have long feared it and the Venetians dubbed it the Devil's Cape. In 1831 the eccentric Sussex landowner John Fuller, or 'Mad Jack' as he was known, built the Belle Tout lighthouse high up on the headland to the west of Beachy Head. The lamp was first lit in 1834 but the lighthouse was never a great success. Its lofty position on the cliff top meant that it was often shrouded in mist and fog and therefore invisible to shipping in the English Channel. A decision was eventually taken to erect a lighthouse at sea level.

Everyone has heard of Beachy Head but not many of us know where the name originates. It comes from the Norman French *Beau Chef* – meaning beautiful headland. The description is certainly apt and this breezy, sprawling cliff top draws visitors and tourists from far and wide who come to marvel at the breathtaking sea views or saunter along the South Downs Way. The whole area is a designated Site of Special Scientific Interest (SSSI).

The walk begins at Birling Gap to the west of Beachy Head. Before long it heads inland, running across the slopes of the South Downs. Within sight of Eastbourne, it suddenly switches direction, following the South Downs Way to Beachy Head and back to Birling Gap. On the way it passes the old Belle Tout lighthouse, now a private home. Whether you walk here in winter or summer, there is always something interesting to add to the enjoyment.

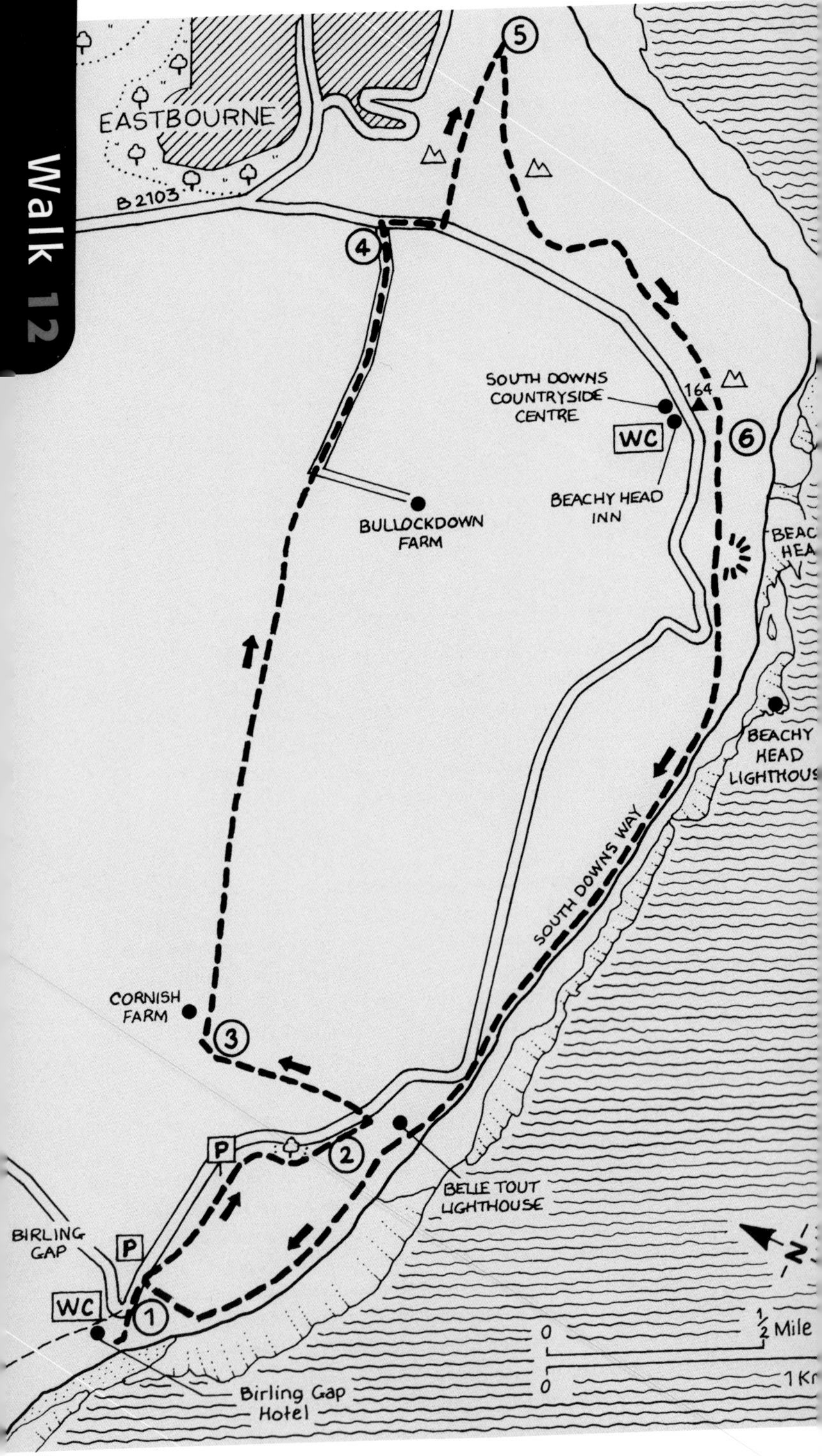

EASTBOURNE

B 2103

⑤

⑥

SOUTH DOWNS
COUNTRYSIDE
CENTRE

164

WC

BEACHY HEAD
INN

BEAC
HEA

BEACHY
HEAD
LIGHTHOUS

BULLOCKDOWN
FARM

SOUTH DOWNS WAY

④

CORNISH
FARM

③

P

②

BELLE TOUT
LIGHTHOUSE

BIRLING
GAP

P

WC

①

N

Birling Gap
Hotel

0   ½ Mile

0   1 Kr

Walk 12 **Directions**

① Walk away from the car park, keeping the road on your left. Ignore the **South Downs Way** sign by the road and continue on the grassy path. Keep to the right of the next car park and follow the path between the trees.

② Keep parallel to the road and, when you see a junction with a concrete track, take the next left path down to meet it. Follow the bridleway signposted '**Cornish Farm and Birling Manor**'. Glance back here for an unexpected view of the old Belle Tout lighthouse. Pass a finger post and continue ahead. Follow the concrete track as it bends right, avoiding the bridleway going straight on. Look for a gate on the right and head east, keeping the fence on your right.

WHILE YOU'RE THERE
Make a point of visiting the **Beachy Head Countryside Centre** which is both educational and entertaining. The centre illustrates the history of the area and its coastline. There are innovative interactive displays on shepherding and Bronze-Age life, touch screen computers and hands-on wildlife displays.

③ Make for another gate and continue ahead. Pass alongside lines of bushes before reaching the next gate. Traffic on the A259 zips by on the skyline. Pass an access track to **Bullockdown Farm** and along here you can see flint walls enclosing fields and pastures.

④ Pass through a gate to the road and turn right, following the wide grassy verge. On reaching two adjoining gates on the right, cross the road and take the grassy path down to a waymarked junction. Follow the path towards **Eastbourne**, signposted '**seafront**', and soon you meet the **South Downs Way**.

⑤ Bear sharp right here and follow the long distance trail as it climbs steadily between bushes and vegetation. Keep right when another path comes in from the left and make for a viewpoint, with the first glimpse of **Beachy Head lighthouse** at the foot of the cliff. Cross the grass, up the slope to the trig point. In front of you now are the **Beachy Head Inn** and **South Downs Countryside Centre**.

WHERE TO EAT AND DRINK
The **Birling Gap Hotel** has a bar, carvery and coffee shop. Dogs are usually welcome in the bar. The busy **Beachy Head Inn** has a bar, restaurant and coffee shop but does not allow dogs.

⑥ Return to the **South Downs Way** and follow it west. The path can be seen ahead, running over the undulating cliff top. Keep the **Belle Tout lighthouse** in your sights and follow the path up towards it. Keep to the right of the old lighthouse and soon the car park at **Birling Gap** edges into view, as do the famous Seven Sisters cliffs. Bear right at the **South Downs Way** post and follow the path down and round to the left. Swing left just before the road and return to the car park at **Birling Gap**.

WHAT TO LOOK FOR
Up on the cliff, above Beachy Head lighthouse, lies the site of a 19th-century **signalling station**. Messages were sent from here to the London offices of Lloyd's confirming the safe arrival of ships and their cargoes. The station closed in 1904.

Holmwood's Highway and its Men

Squatters and smugglers, highwaymen and a hero – Holmwood has them all!

•DISTANCE•	3¼ miles (5.3km)
•MINIMUM TIME•	1hr 15min
•ASCENT / GRADIENT•	164ft (50m) ▲▲▲
•LEVEL OF DIFFICULTY•	
•PATHS•	Forest and farm tracks, muddy in places, some minor roads
•LANDSCAPE•	Wooded common, with clearings and scattered houses
•SUGGESTED MAP•	aqua3 OS Explorer 146 Dorking, Box Hill & Reigate
•START / FINISH•	Grid reference: TQ 183454
•DOG FRIENDLINESS•	Welcome on Holmwood Common, please remember to poop scoop, especially in car park area
•PARKING•	National Trust car park at Fourwents Pond
•PUBLIC TOILETS•	None on route

BACKGROUND TO THE WALK

Visit Holmwood today and you'll find a peaceful tangle of woodland, bracken and grass, with several decent car parks and the placid Fourwents Pond glistening calmly in the south east corner of the common. Pretty much what you'd expect, really, from an area that's been in the hands of the National Trust since 1956. Nevertheless, the common has a rather more turbulent history than you might guess.

Holmwood was part of the Manor of Dorking and was held by King Harold until William took over at the time of the Norman conquest. Perhaps the area had little to interest the Conqueror; at that time Holmwood was something of a wasteland, and it didn't even get a mention in the Domesday Book.

Use It or Lose It

By the Middle Ages, squatters had begun to move in. They built makeshift houses, grazed a few animals, and cleared the woodland for timber and fuel. The new residents also went in for sheep stealing and smuggling, as well as the more honest trade of making brooms.

Smuggling remained rife well into the 18th century. Nearby Leith Hill tower was used for signalling during the 1770s, and the bootleggers also met in pubs and cottages on the common itself. One of these, the Old Nag's Head, once stood on the corner of Holmwood View Road and the A24 (Point **Ⓓ** on the map). Brook Lodge Farm, just up the road from Fourwents Pond, stands on the site of another smugglers' haunt; the old Bottle and Glass.

Just Passing Through

Meanwhile, efforts were being made to improve local communications, which had become rather worse than when the Romans drove the road which became Stane Street across the common on its way from London to Chichester. In 1755 a turnpike road was built on the line of the modern A24, and up to 18 coaches a day began rolling through Holmwood. As a result, highwaymen prospered here until well into the 19th century.

American Millionaire

But the new road had its fair share of gentlemen, too. The American millionaire Alfred Gwynne Vanderbilt regularly drove his coach along this stretch, and he made many English friends. He died tragically in May 1915, when the Cunard liner *Lusitania* was torpedoed by a German U-boat off the southern coast of Ireland. Gallant to the last, Vanderbilt is said to have helped search for children on the sinking ship, and gave his own lifebelt to an elderly lady passenger.

You can see Vanderbilt's simple granite memorial, erected on his favourite road by a few of his British coaching friends and admirers, by making a short diversion along the roadside pavement from South Holmwood and crossing near the bus shelter.

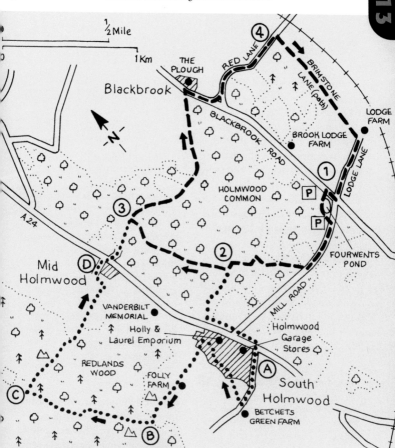

Walk 13 Directions

① Head out of the car park towards **Fourwents Pond**, and bear right along the waterside track, keeping the pond on your left. At the far corner of the pond, cross a small plank bridge, walk through the smaller car park, and turn right into **Mill Road**. After 400yds (366m), turn right up the lane signposted '**Gable End, Applegarth and Went Cottage**'; then, 30yds (27m) further on, fork left on to the waymarked public footpath.

Walk 13

Continue under a set of power lines, then follow the blue waymarks across the parting of two rough gravel tracks before re-crossing one of them at another blue waymark. Follow the path to the next waymarker post and swing left at the yellow arrow that points your way to **Clematis Cottage**. Turn right here, and join the gravelled track as far as **Uplands Cottage**.

② Turn left for 20yds (18m), then slip away to the right on to a grassy footpath. At the end of the footpath turn right, dodge through a wooden post and rail barrier, then turn left at the blue and yellow waymarker post, 25yds (23m) further on. Fork

right at the next junction of paths to a clearing in the woods and drop down the grassy slope straight ahead, now following the blue waymarked route on to a gravelled surface at the foot of the hill. After 300yds (274m), keep a sharp eye out for a blue and yellow waymarker to the left of the path, and turn right here, on to another gravelled path.

③ This yellow waymarked route leads purposefully across the **Common** beside the National Trust estate boundary, and brings you out opposite the **Plough** pub at Blackbrook. Turn right on to **Blackbrook Road**, then left into **Red Lane** (signposted towards Leigh and Brockham) and follow it for about ½ mile (800m).

④ Turn right into **Brimstone Lane** at the public bridleway signpost. Continue through a five-bar gate and down the right-hand side of an open field, leaving through a second gate at the far end. Follow the track as far as **Lodge Farm**, then turn right on to **Lodge Lane**, which leads you back to the **Fourwents Pond**. Turn right here, for the last 100yds (91m) back to the start.

Redlands Wood Loop

Extend your time at Holmwood with this loop in quiet woodlands.
See map and information panel for Walk 13

•DISTANCE•	6 miles (9.7km)
•MINIMUM TIME•	2hrs 30min
•ASCENT / GRADIENT•	607ft (185m) ▲▲▲
•LEVEL OF DIFFICULTY•	

Walk 14 Directions (Walk 13 option)

Leave Walk 13 at Point ②, and turn left on to a grassy track. After 300yds (274m) it swings to the right and comes to a crossroads. Turn left, and continue towards the busy A24 until the roadside houses come into view; then bear left, and walk parallel to the main road. Continue past **Mill Road** to the war memorial, then cross the main road via the subway, Point Ⓐ.

Now take the quiet lane up towards **Betchets Green Farm**. Fork right just beyond the farm, and turn sharp right at the public footpath sign 75yds (69m) further on. Follow the path over two stiles, bear left into **Warwick Close**, and continue until the road ends at a public bridleway. Turn left, walk past Folly Farm, and begin climbing towards **Redlands Wood**, Point Ⓑ.

After 450yds (411m) you'll come to a rough forest ride. Turn right, and continue up the hill until the ride swings left to a five-way junction. Think of it as a mini-roundabout, and take the third exit. You'll climb briefly, before dropping to a forest crossroads, Point Ⓒ.

Turn right, then right again at the blue waymark arrow. Keep straight ahead at the junction 130yds (119m) further on, now following the yellow waymarker. At the bottom of the hill swing right over a brook; then, almost at once, fork left on to a narrow footpath just inside the woodland edge. A stile leads you out of the woods and across an open field to another stile. Nip over this and continue following the track as it zig-zags left and right into **Norfolk Lane**, back to the A24, Point Ⓓ.

Cross the dual carriageway with care and walk down **Holmwood View Road**. Continue along the grassy footpath at the bottom to rejoin the main route at Point ③.

WHAT TO LOOK FOR ⓘ
You may just be lucky enough to spot one or two of the shy **roe deer** that live in Redlands Wood. At around 25in (65cm) at the shoulder, these graceful creatures are smaller than the more common fallow deer, which grow to around 3ft (90cm) tall. The young roe fawns have a dappled coat but, unlike fallow deer, the adults are never spotted; their coats are foxy red in summer, toning down to a dark grey-brown in winter. Look out, too, for their distinctive two-toed footprints or 'slots' in the muddier parts of the forest.

Walk 15

Scratchwood's Surprising Open Space

An ideal point to stop and stretch the legs if you are driving along the A1 or about to join the M1.

•DISTANCE•	2 miles (3.2km)
•MINIMUM TIME•	1hr
•ASCENT / GRADIENT•	98ft (30m)
•LEVEL OF DIFFICULTY•	
•PATHS•	Gravel paths and forest tracks
•LANDSCAPE•	Woodland
•SUGGESTED MAP•	aqua3 OS Explorer 173 London North
•START / FINISH•	Grid reference: TQ 207949
•DOG FRIENDLINESS•	No problems
•PARKING•	Car park off northbound carriageway of A1, 1 mile (1.6km) north of Apex Corner
•PUBLIC TOILETS•	At car park

Walk 15 Directions

As you'll see from the information board, there are three marked trails here: red, blue and yellow. You can choose your own route or follow this one, which is a combination of the red and blue trails.

Head for the track at the far, right-hand corner of the car park, near the kiosk, and follow this path, part of the **London Loop**, through a metal gate. Take the right-hand fork, cross a footbridge over a ditch and follow the path uphill along the central path ahead.

The ancient woodland of Scratchwood can be traced back to the last ice age, when it was part of the Middlesex Forest. Although it first appeared on maps from the 16th century, other documents name it at least 300 years before that. Many landowners built large

houses in the area. In 1866 the Cox family bought a 1,000 acre (405ha) estate, which included Scratchwood. The area was used for game-rearing and field sports. Later the woodland management focused on producing oak timber. The relatively small woodland area of Scratchwood that you see today is mostly a result of the incursion of the A1 Barnet bypass, which, in 1927, sliced through the site separating it from Moat Mount, on the opposite side of the dual carriageway.

A few paces further on, the path swings to the right and then descends, crossing another path and a footbridge before dipping and ascending once more. Follow the path to the right as it crosses another footbridge. About 50yds (46m) further, at a wooden post marked red, turn left along a path that later narrows and descends gradually. Here you will see large clumps of rhododendron. These were introduced, but, given half a chance, grow at a tremendous speed and have a tendency to eliminate all other ground vegetation. Careful woodland management, undertaken by Barnet borough council, has been necessary to enable other species to survive. Elsewhere the ancient ground cover – such as bracken, bramble and ivy – can be seen. Most of the large trees in these woods are oaks, but you will also see other typical English woodland trees including hornbeam, hazel, birch, holly and wild cherry.

> **WHERE TO EAT AND DRINK** ℹ️
> Less than 2 miles away (3.2km) is the village of Arkley and, by a roundabout off the A411, is the **Arkley Arms**. Despite its bland exterior it is well worth the short detour. It's relaxed – more like a hotel lounge than a traditional pub – with a mix of chairs, armchairs and sofas, and open fireplaces that have logs stacked symmetrically at the side. Subtle lighting, off-beat paintings and a warm colour scheme add to the designer interior. Although dogs are not allowed inside, they are welcome outside where water is often provided.

> **WHILE YOU'RE THERE** ℹ️
> If you are a **model plane** enthusiast, take yours with you for the route takes you past a field where model aircraft are sometimes flown. The grass is kept short, by a combination of rabbits and mowing.

At a clearing leading down to an embankment, turn left. A little further on you'll pass more wooden posts, marked blue. As the path rises again bear sharp left at another post and turn right down steps and over a brook. Continue ahead as the path rises to another post and some more steps leading to a footbridge.

If you are walking here in the summer, you may hear the call of a jay. You may also catch the sound of a woodpecker – three different types have been spotted in Scratchwood. There have also been regular sightings of nuthatches and treecreepers on the tree trunks. The rough, bushy areas attract warblers and, in winter, redwings feed on berries. Insects too are attracted by the wide variety of habitats in Scratchwood, where on bright, sunny days you will see large numbers of butterflies and dragonflies. Be careful not to tread on any of the giant stag beetles you may see scuttling across the path; they are now a protected species.

The path passes three more posts and after the last, it rejoins the **London Loop**. The field to the south of the entrance was once a hay meadow, used for feeding some of London's large number of horses. At the footbridge, turn right along the limestone scalpings track back to the car park.

> **WHAT TO LOOK FOR** ℹ️
> Spare a thought for London's **woodlands** while walking through Scratchwood. For 5,000 years tree numbers fell consistently, making way for farms and land to grow crops. But, due to increased industrialisation and a shift towards city living, England now has as many trees as it did in the time of Robin Hood. That's roughly 25 trees for every man, woman and child in the country. The devastation seen after the 1987 storms made many people realise how much they took the landscape for granted. In fact, earlier in the 1980s the Forestry Commission was spending just £800,000 per year on planting new trees, but by 2000 this had risen to £9.7m. Robin Hood's merry men wouldn't find it difficult to hide in this area of woodland.

Walk 16

Bracing Bradwell-on-Sea

Smugglers, sea walls and a dying nuclear power station.

•DISTANCE•	6 miles (9.7km)
•MINIMUM TIME•	3hrs
•ASCENT / GRADIENT•	Negligible
•LEVEL OF DIFFICULTY•	
•PATHS•	Stony and grassy paths with some road walking
•LANDSCAPE•	Mudflats, salt marshes, beach, farmland, sea wall and nuclear power station
•SUGGESTED MAP•	aqua3 OS Explorer 176 Blackwater Estuary, Maldon
•START / FINISH•	Grid reference: TM 024078
•DOG FRIENDLINESS•	A beach for a good romp and paddle; nuclear power station provides a poop bin
•PARKING•	Informal parking at entrance to footpath at East Hall Farm and free car park at Bradwell Nuclear Power Station
•PUBLIC TOILETS•	Visitor Centre at Bradwell Nuclear Power Station

BACKGROUND TO THE WALK

If you yearn for huge skies, bracing sea air and long yellow sands, with not a lilo or brolly in sight, then this walk is for you. The Dengie (sounds like Benjie) Peninsula, a vast area of pancake-flat marshes and arable farmland, really does seem in a world of its own, its haunting beauty attracting those seeking to escape the stresses of modern city life.

Smugglers' Haunts
The Dengie Peninsula is bounded by the estuaries of the River Blackwater to the north and the River Crouch to the south. Yet for all its isolation, jutting out into the dove-grey waters of the North Sea, it was a place that needed defending. The Romans built a fort where the present Chapel of St Peter's-on-the-Wall stands, one of several along the coast built to fend off raiders. In the 18th and 19th centuries the chapel took on a different role as a hiding place for bands of smugglers, who would use it to store crates of whisky and rum and other contraband. Meanwhile, notable Bradwell residents, such as Hezekiah Staines, played part-time policeman by day and criminal by night, and spread rumours that the chapel was haunted. Maybe it is.

Contraband Course
This walk starts on an isolated pathway leading to the Chapel of St Peter's-on-the-Wall, the oldest church still in use in England and certainly the sole monument to Celtic Christianity in Essex. Built by the missionary St Cedd in AD 654 it is almost entirely made from debris from the Roman fort on which it stands. In 1920 it took on its present name, and since 1948 has attracted pilgrims from all over the world. Each summer, services are held in the simple barn-like interior. If you choose to take this walk on a cold winter's day when the skies are white and the mists cast a ghostly shroud over the bleak windswept marshes, it's a perfect place for taking shelter from the elements. Once through the heavy wooden door you can imagine old smugglers stacking up their ill-gotten goods inside.

Perhaps the most incongruous blot on the landscape, as you continue along the sea wall to Bradwell Waterside, is the looming grey, grim blocks of Bradwell Nuclear Power Station, visible for miles around. It started life in 1962, but costs of continued operation now outweigh its earning potential, and the site is due to be decommissioned. You can take refreshment at the Green Man pub, a smugglers' haven in its day, before continuing to Bradwell-on-Sea, in truth a good way from the seaside. And to complete the contraband course, pause at the parish church where miscreants were incarcerated in a tiny square cell, the Cage, or punished at the whipping post.

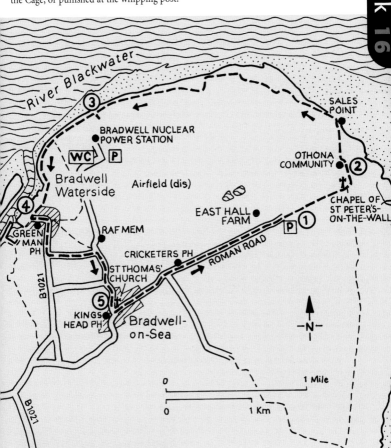

Walk 16 **Directions**

① Take the wide grassy path from the car park towards the sea and in ½ mile (800m) reach the ancient **Chapel of St Peter's-on-the-Wall**. Continue walking towards the sea for another 30yds (27m) and turn left at the T-junction. After

100yds (91m) climb the wooden steps to the sea defence wall.

② At the fingerpost marking the religious community of Othona, turn right and walk along the wall with the sea on your right. For the next 2 miles (3.2km) your route remains on top of the sea wall, mainly a firm, grassy path

Walk 16

punctuated with areas of concrete. On your left, and sometimes seemingly at a lower level to the sea, is private farmland. On your right, salt marsh gives way to white sand and shingle and extensive mudflats at low tide. The seashore makes a lovely detour but at high tide you have to remain on the concrete path. There are good views across the Blackwater estuary to Mersea Island. On the seaward side of the path there are concrete pill boxes, relics of World War Two. The second pill box marks **Sales Point**, from where there are views of the mooring area used by Thames sailing barges. Follow the path for a mile (1.6km) and you can see the framework of the beacon, a good place for spotting swooping cormorants.

> ### WHERE TO EAT AND DRINK ⓘ
> A rather limited choice confined to public houses. Take your pick from the **Cricketers** in Roman Road, the **Green Man** at Bradwell Waterside, or the **Kings Head** at Bradwell-on-Sea which has displays of old photographs of the area and a pair of llamas in the backyard to amuse the children.

Road with the marina on your right. Sean Connery, Bobby Moore and Roger Moore had a hand in turning this marina into a business venture in the 1960s. Continue past the marina and turn left into **Trusses Road**. At the T-junction, turn right towards **Bradwell-on-Sea** (a left turn here towards Bradwell Nuclear Power Station will take you to the RAF memorial at Bradwell Bay Airfield).

⑤ At Bradwell-on-Sea follow the **High Street** to its junction with **East End Road** where, on the corner, you will find St Thomas' Church opposite the **Kings Head** pub. Pass **Caidge Cottages** on your left, the village school on your right and continue for about a mile (1.6km) along the straight **Roman Road**, with maybe a stop at the **Cricketers** pub, before reaching the car park.

> ### WHILE YOU'RE THERE ⓘ
> You can't help but notice the huge power station on the route which shut down in March 2002 after 40 years of service. When working it generated enough electricity each day to meet the needs of three towns the size of Chelmsford, Colchester and Southend put together.

③ In 1.5 miles (2.4km) the bulk of **Bradwell Nuclear Power Station** is upon you. You may either continue on the route by the coast or make a detour to take in the nature trail around the station. However our route continues along the sea wall to **Bradwell Waterside**.

④ At the jetty, turn left on to **Waterside Road** keeping the yacht club and **Green Man** pub on your right. Continue along **Waterside**

> ### WHAT TO LOOK FOR ⓘ
> Look for the **war memorial** beside the disused airfield perimeter track at Bradwell-on-Sea. Surrounded by remembrance poppies, it is in the form of a battleship grey Mosquito aircraft appearing to plunge into the ground and is a poignant reminder of those pilots who never returned from operations during World War Two.

From Sunny Southwold and its Pier

Around this old-fashioned holiday resort on an island surrounded by river, creek and sea.

Walk 17

•DISTANCE•	4 miles (6.4km)
•MINIMUM TIME•	1hr 30min
•ASCENT / GRADIENT•	Negligible ▲▲ ▲▲
•LEVEL OF DIFFICULTY•	
•PATHS•	Riverside paths, seaside promenade, town streets, 2 stiles
•LANDSCAPE•	Southwold and its surroundings – river, marshes, coast
•SUGGESTED MAP•	aqua3 OS Explorer 231 Southwold & Bungay
•START / FINISH•	Grid reference: TM 511766
•DOG FRIENDLINESS•	Most of walk suitable for dogs off leads
•PARKING•	Beach car park (pay-and-display) or free in nearby streets
•PUBLIC TOILETS•	Beside pier, near beach and car park at Southwold Harbour

BACKGROUND TO THE WALK

The arrival of the first steamboats for more than 70 years marked a return to the glory days for Southwold Pier in the summer of 2002. The pier was originally built in 1899, when Southwold was a flourishing Victorian holiday resort. Mixed bathing had just been introduced on the beach, on condition that men and women were kept at least 20yds (18m) apart and changed in separate 'bathing machines' into costumes which covered their bodies from neck to knees. The *Belle* steamer brought holidaymakers on its daily voyage from London and the pier was a hive of activity as porters unloaded their cases and carried them to their lodgings.

Pleasure Pier

The T-end, where the boats docked, was swept away in a storm in 1934. During World War Two, the pier was split in two as a precaution against a German invasion. By the time Chris and Helen Iredale bought the pier in 1987, storms and neglect had reduced it to a rotting hulk. Years later, the couple have realised their dream of rebuilding and reopening the pier, so that visitors can once again stroll along the boardwalk with the sea spray in their faces and watch the boats unloading their passengers at a new landing stage.

Old-fashioned Fun

An exhibition on the pier tells the history of the seaside holiday, complete with saucy postcards, kitsch teapots, palm readers, end-of-the-pier shows, high-diving 'professors' and old-style arcade machines – such as the 'kiss-meter' where you can find out whether you are flirtatious, amorous, frigid or sexy. A separate pavilion contains modern machines by local inventor Tim Hunkin, who also designed the ingenious water clock, with chimes and special effects every half-hour. You can eat ice cream or fish and chips, drink a pint of the local beer, play pool in the amusement arcade or watch the fishermen while taking in the sea air. Especially in summer, the pier provides a focus for good old-fashioned fun.

Walk 17

Not So Brash

Southwold, situated on an island between the River Blyth and the sea, is one of those genteel, low-key seaside resorts where, in spite of the pier, everything is done in good taste. Make no mistake, this is a popular spot but it has none of the brashness of kiss-me-quick Felixstowe or Lowestoft. The character of Southwold seems to be summed up by the rows of brightly-coloured beach huts on the seafront promenade – some of which have been sold for the price of a three-bedroom cottage elsewhere – and the peaceful greens with their Georgian and Edwardian houses. Adnams brewery dominates the town and it is no surprise to discover that the beer is still delivered to pubs on horse-drawn drays. Southwold is that sort of place.

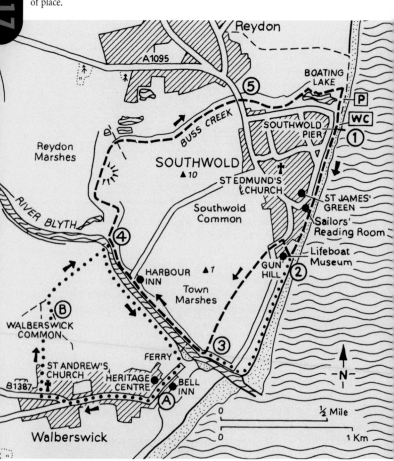

Walk 17 **Directions**

① Leave the pier and turn left along the seafront, either following the promenade past the beach huts and climbing some steps or walking along the clifftop path with views

over the beach. After passing **St James' Green**, where a pair of cannon stand either side of a mast, continue along the clifftop path to **Gun Hill**, where six more cannon, captured at the Battle of Culloden near Inverness in 1746, can be seen facing out to sea.

Walk 17

② From Gun Hill, head inland alongside the large **South Green**, then turn left along **Queen's Road** to the junction with **Gardner Road**. Cross this road and look for the **Ferry Path** footpath, that follows a stream beside the marshes as it heads towards the river. Alternatively, stay on the clifftop path and walk across the dunes until you reach the mouth of the **River Blyth**.

WHERE TO EAT AND DRINK

There are numerous cafés and restaurants in Southwold, many of them specialising in fresh local fish. **Sutherland House**, on the High Street, serves fresh fish and game in the setting of an Elizabethan merchant's house, used by the Duke of York (later James II), Lord High Admiral of England, as his headquarters during the Battle of Sole Bay, when the British and Dutch fleets clashed off Southwold in 1672. Among the pubs serving Adnams beer are the **Sole Bay Inn**, a Victorian pub opposite the brewery on East Green, and the **Red Lion** on South Green. Another good choice is the **Harbour Inn**, beside the river at the halfway point of the walk.

WHAT TO LOOK FOR

It's worth a visit to the cathedral-like **St Edmund's Church**, whose 100ft (30m) flint tower stands guard over the town. The greatest treasure here is the 15th-century rood screen which spans the width of the church, a riot of colour as vivid as when it was painted, with angels in glory and a set of panels depicting the twelve apostles.

③ Turn right and walk beside the river, passing the Walberswick ferry, a group of fishing huts where fresh fish is sold, and the **Harbour Inn**. After about ¾ mile (1.2km) you reach an iron bridge on the site of the old Southwold-to-Halesworth railway line.

④ Keep ahead at the bridge, crossing a stile and following the path right alongside **Buss Creek** to make a circuit of the island. There are good views to Southwold, dominated by the lighthouse and the tower of St Edmund's Church. Horses and cattle can often be seen grazing on the marshes. Keep straight ahead at a four-finger signpost and stay on the raised path to reach a white-painted bridge.

⑤ Climb up to the road and cross the bridge, then continue on the path beside **Buss Creek**. The path skirts a lake on its way down to the sea. Turn right and walk across the car park to return to the pier.

Extending the Walk

You can extend this walk by catching the ferry (in summer) at Point ③ to **Walberswick**. A right turn past the church will lead you on to heathland where you can pick up a track back to the riverside. Cross the bridge to rejoin the main walk at Point ④ or turn right to walk along the riverbank back to the ferry.

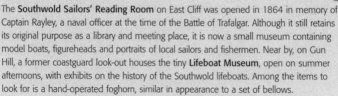

WHILE YOU'RE THERE

The **Southwold Sailors' Reading Room** on East Cliff was opened in 1864 in memory of Captain Rayley, a naval officer at the time of the Battle of Trafalgar. Although it still retains its original purpose as a library and meeting place, it is now a small museum containing model boats, figureheads and portraits of local sailors and fishermen. Near by, on Gun Hill, a former coastguard look-out houses the tiny **Lifeboat Museum**, open on summer afternoons, with exhibits on the history of the Southwold lifeboats. Among the items to look for is a hand-operated foghorn, similar in appearance to a set of bellows.

A Merrie Tale of Sherwood Forest

Enjoy a fascinating and enchanting walk among the age-old oaks of this legendary forest.

•DISTANCE•	5½ miles (8.8km)
•MINIMUM TIME•	2hrs 30min
•ASCENT / GRADIENT•	278ft (85m)
•LEVEL OF DIFFICULTY•	
•PATHS•	Easy woodland tracks and wide forest rides
•LANDSCAPE•	Beautiful mixed woodland, more open to north
•SUGGESTED MAP•	aqua3 OS Explorer 270 Sherwood Forest
•START / FINISH•	Grid reference: SK 626676
•DOG FRIENDLINESS•	On lead around visitor centre, otherwise excellent
•PARKING•	Sherwood Forest Visitor Centre (pay-and-display)
•PUBLIC TOILETS•	Sherwood Forest Visitor Centre

BACKGROUND TO THE WALK

If Robin Hood or one of his merrie men were to return to Sherwood Forest today they would no doubt be surprised at how dramatically it has shrunk. The modern Sherwood Forest Country Park covers 450 acres (182ha), whereas the original area was more like 100,000 acres (40,500ha). But there again this vast ancient forest, which at the time of the Norman Conquest covered most of Nottinghamshire north of the River Trent, was not in fact a blanket forest but a mix of wood, heathland and scrub. It was the preserve of the nobility, where the king and his entourage hunted deer, and the commoners were subject to strict Forest Laws that could see a man's hand cut off for poaching.

Mighty Oaks from Little Acorns Grow

In England and Wales 'ancient woodland' generally refers to woods that have existed since 1600 (1750 in Scotland). Here at Sherwood the surviving woodland, though small, is a wonderful mix of native broadleaved varieties, dominated by oak and birch. Both varieties of native British oak can be found in the forest – common or English oak, and sessile or durmast oak – while newer conifer plantations extend the tree cover east and west.

The ancient woodland is full of light and atmosphere, and the highlight is surely the gigantic old oak trees that pepper the forest. There are over 900 trees above 600 years old (sometimes known as 'druids'), and while a few are simply gnarled and hollow old stumps, others still dominate the surroundings with their massive 'stag heads' of twisted limbs and spreading foliage. The most famous of these is the Major Oak, visited on this walk, and one of the largest trees in England. Its exact age is somewhat uncertain, estimates having varied over the years from 500 to 1,500 years, but there's no doubting its sheer size. The hollow trunk is 33ft (10m) in circumference, and such is the spread of its colossal branches (92ft/28m) that they have to be propped up with artificial supports. But whether even the Major Oak's hollow trunk could have hidden Robin Hood and his entire band of merrie men, as legend has it, is rather more doubtful.

A Changing Landscape

The evolution of Sherwood Forest over the last millennium has seen it change from its original role as a royal hunting ground to a source of valuable raw material. English oak was much in demand by a range of eager consumers, from shipbuilders and furniture-makers to miners and charcoal burners. Between 1609 and 1790 the number of Sherwood's oaks plummeted by 80 per cent. Today only 11.6 per cent of the United Kingdom's land area is covered by woodland. In other countries in the European Union, the average tree cover is around 36 per cent.

To find out more about Sherwood Forest, and about Britain's valuable woodland assets, make sure you take some time to explore the visitor centre before or after your walk.

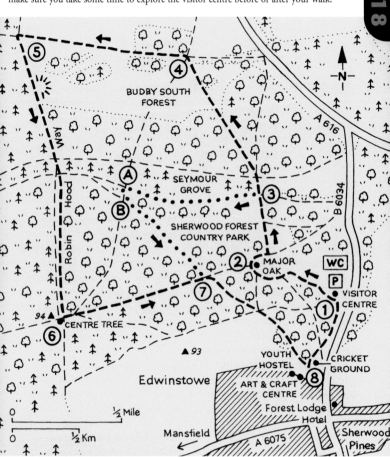

Walk 18 **Directions**

① Facing the main entrance to **Sherwood Forest Visitor Centre** from the car park, turn left and follow the well-signposted route to the **Major Oak**.

② Go along the curving path as it completes a semi-circle around the impressive old tree and continue as far as the junction with a public bridleway (signposted). Turn left here and walk this straight and uncomplicated route for ¼ mile (400m), ignoring all paths off.

Walk 18

③ At a green notice board, warning of a nearby military training area, the main path bears left. Instead go straight ahead, past the metal bar gate, for a path that continues over a crossroads to become a wide, fenced track through pleasant open country of heather and bracken known as **Budby South Forest**.

④ At the very far side go through a gate and turn left on to an unmade lane, and walk this undulating route

for ¾ mile (1.2km).

⑤ At the major junction just before the plantation begins, turn left, indicated 'Centre Tree'. With the rows of conifers on your right, and good views across **Budby South Forest** on your left, keep to this straight and obvious track. Where the track divides into two parallel trails, the gravelly track on the right is technically the cycle route, while the more leafy and grassy ride to the left is the bridleway, but either can be used.

⑥ When you reach the **Centre Tree** – a huge spreading oak – the two

routes converge to continue past a bench down a wide avenue among the trees. Don't go down this but instead turn left and, ignoring paths off right and left, carry straight on along the main track back into the heart of the forest.

⑦ After almost ¾ mile (1.2km) you pass a metal bar gate on the right and then meet a bridleway coming in from the left. Ignoring the inviting path straight ahead (which returns to the Major Oak) bear right on the main track, past some bare holes and dips hollowed out by children's bikes. At a large junction of criss-crossing routes go straight on (signposted 'Fairground') so that an open field and distant housing become visible to your right. This wide sandy track descends to a field by Edwinstowe **cricket ground**. The **Art and Craft Centre** and youth hostel are on the far side, and the village centre beyond.

⑧ To return to the **visitor centre** and car park, follow the well-walked, signposted track back up

A Shorter Sherwood Forest Walk

This easier option is ideal for those after the gentlest of strolls.
See map and information panel for Walk 18

•DISTANCE•	3¼ miles (5.3km)
•MINIMUM TIME•	1hr 30min
•ASCENT / GRADIENT•	164ft (50m)
•LEVEL OF DIFFICULTY•	

Walk 19 Directions (Walk 18 option)

At Point ③ follow the main track as it bends left by the green notice board entitled 'Dukeries Training Area' and carry on along this wide and obvious route. To the right is **Seymour Grove**, a coniferous plantation that is in stark contrast to the more mixed and attractive oak woodland to your left. Look out for several old oak trunks, hollow and slowly rotting, but still awesome in their size. How old do you think they are? One of the problems with accurately ageing the Major Oak is that experts believe that over the centuries several different oak trees may have fused into the one main specimen that is seen today.

After roughly ⅔ mile (1.1km) turn left on to a clear public footpath (Point Ⓐ), then in a few paces branch left again on a short linking path to join a major bridleway leftwards (Point Ⓑ). If you accidentally over-shoot the first turning you will meet the signposted bridleway 300yds (274m) further up the path, and so turn sharp left here and follow this route back and stay on it.

The bridleway heads south eastwards through the heart of the forest, via open glades and groves of silver birch. Little paths disappear off into the trees, and it is easy to imagine a small band of outlaws vanishing into the woodland without a trace. In medieval times the forest would almost certainly have played host to such gangs, but whether they were led by Robin of Locksley is another matter.

After a little under ½ mile (800m) you reach a junction of tracks (Point ⑦). From here continue straight on to resume the main route, or turn left for a short path back to the Major Oak and the visitors' centre beyond.

WHAT TO LOOK FOR

The annual **Robin Hood Festival** takes place during the summer holidays, when the visitor centre puts on a variety of themed events – from archery and jousting to falconry and entertainers. A permanent display at the centre also explains more about day-to-day life in a medieval forest, and the 'Forests of the World' exhibition takes a closer look at the ecology of a woodland.

Walk 20

Wainfleet's Honest Ales

A short wander around a Lincolnshire market town famous for its brewery.

•DISTANCE•	3¼ miles (5.3km)
•MINIMUM TIME•	1hr 45min
•ASCENT / GRADIENT•	Negligible
•LEVEL OF DIFFICULTY•	
•PATHS•	Straightforward field paths and lanes
•LANDSCAPE•	Flat coastal plain dominated by arable fields
•SUGGESTED MAP•	aqua3 OS Explorer 274 Skegness, Alford & Spilsby
•START / FINISH•	Grid reference: TF 498589
•DOG FRIENDLINESS•	Very good, apart from one field with cows at end
•PARKING•	Market Square, Wainfleet town centre
•PUBLIC TOILETS•	Brook's Walk, opposite Market Place

Walk 20 Directions

The early growth of Wainfleet, south of Skegness, was the result of a combination of medieval salt-workings and the presence of a safe haven for boats – 'fleet' was once a Roman term to denote a navigable creek.

Facing the **Woolpack Hotel** by Market Place in the centre of Wainfleet, turn left. Walk along the main road and over the level crossing, then turn right for a signposted public footpath just beyond **Barton Road**. This narrow, semi-surfaced route passes a new housing development and, beyond a footbridge, heads out across open fields where staple vegetables such as cabbages and potatoes are often grown. Continue all the way to the

> **WHERE TO EAT AND DRINK** ⓘ
> The **Woolpack Hotel** serves food every lunchtime and evening. The **All Saints Church shop** serves tea and coffee Monday to Saturday, and refreshments are also served at **Magdalene Museum**.

far side and turn left on to a lane. In 100yds (91m) go right on a waymarked footpath along the back of houses, and finally join the riverside lane on the far side of another small field.

Turn right and walk alongside the **Steeping River**, either on the lane or, better still, on top of the grassy embankment above.

At **Crow's Bridge** cross over to the road on the south side, and turn left (downstream) on **Haven Bank**. If you want to lengthen the walk you could continue beyond Crow's Bridge as far as **Wainfleet Bank**, crossing over to the **Barkham Arms**, a pub with limited evening opening times that caters mainly for the adjoining caravan park. Near by is the site of the medieval village of Wainfleet, and a footpath across the fields connects with the now isolated St Mary's Church. Return along the opposite bank.

The quiet lane downstream from Crow's Bridge passes a stretch popular with local anglers then, after the road veers away from the river through houses and a pavement appears, it bends sharply left. Go straight on here, along a narrow walkway between dense hedges, then out behind a row of back gardens. Cross the end of a drive and, after a small fenced strip, emerge on to a road by **Half Penny Hill Cottage**.

> **WHILE YOU'RE THERE** ⓘ
> The **Steeping River** issues out into the North Sea at Gibraltar Point. This remote location, reached by a no through road south from Skegness, is an important National Nature Reserve. Its extensive salt marsh, mudflats and sand-dune system supports a wide variety of wildlife.

Turn right, then in 220yds (201m) go left into **St Michael's Lane**. Walk past the converted stump of an old windmill and, after the last house on the left, turn left between hedges and out across the middle of a field on a popular local path. Continue around the cricket pitch to the stile on the far side, then head half right through the overgrown parkland of **Wainfleet Hall**. Go out of the gate on the far side and turn left to walk the pavement of **Boston Road** back into the town. Just over the bridge you reach **Batemans Brewery** on the left, off **Mill Lane** – depending on the wind direction, you'll probably smell the hops first.

The award-winning Batemans Brewery is a must-see for any real-ale lover or pub-goer, and even the non-enthusiast may be surprised at how fascinating the place can be. Established in 1874, Batemans is still run by the same family, and the visitors' centre (open daily) has a comprehensible, step-by-step guide to the brewing process. Discover how a mash tun works, the secrets

of wort-cooling, and why the cask-sniffer does what he does. The exhibition also includes a huge collection of beer and pub memorabilia – from a range of traditional pub games, beer mats and posters, to the largest collection of beer bottles in the world (over 4,500 different specimens at the last count). There are organised tours of the brewhouse every afternoon, and in the Windmill Bar you can sample the real thing – or tea and coffee if you prefer.

Continue back along the main road to the railway crossing. On the near side is **All Saints** parish church with its unusual bell turret and, on the far side, turn right into **Silver Street**. Rounding the far bend you arrive at **Magdalene Museum**. The impressive, turreted building was built in 1484 for Magdalene College School, and now houses the local library and museum (open each afternoon, except Monday and Wednesday, from Easter to the end of September).

Carry on along what has now become **St John's Street**, and on past the junction at the end by **Market Place** to turn left into **Barkham Street** – and what must surely be the most unexpected encounter on the whole walk (see What to Look For). Turn left at the far end of Barkham Street to return to **Market Place**.

> **WHAT TO LOOK FOR** ⓘ
> **Barkham Street**, near Market Place, was built in 1847 by the Governors of Bethlem Hospital. It's an exact replica of a three-storeyed, terraced row of London houses that they had constructed around the hospital in Southwark, and apparently the design was unchanged for small-town Lincolnshire in order to cut costs!

All Around The Wrekin

A Shropshire classic with added value – The Wrekin and The Ercall.

·DISTANCE·	8½ miles (13.7km)
·MINIMUM TIME·	3hrs
·ASCENT / GRADIENT·	1,585ft (485m) ▲▲▲
·LEVEL OF DIFFICULTY·	
·PATHS·	Woodland footpaths, urban streets, quiet lanes, 2 stiles
·LANDSCAPE·	Hills and woods on edge of Wellington
·SUGGESTED MAP·	aqua3 OS Explorer 242 Telford, Ironbridge & The Wrekin
·START / FINISH·	Grid reference: SJ 651113
·DOG FRIENDLINESS·	Dog heaven, except on firing days (See note below)
·PARKING·	Belmont or Swimming Pool East car parks, both on Tan Bank, off Victoria Road, Wellington
·PUBLIC TOILETS·	Victoria Street car park, between bus and train stations
·NOTE·	Rifle range on The Wrekin – warning notices posted, but take care on firing days

BACKGROUND TO THE WALK

Those who live in Shropshire know that The Wrekin is more than just a hill. For all true Salopians it is a sort of focal point and symbol of Shropshire, the embodiment of home, a sentiment implied in the traditional toast 'To all friends around The Wrekin'. Although it reaches only a modest 1,323ft (407m), its splendid isolation makes it seem higher. This illusion is strengthened by its shape: while basically a whaleback, it appears conical from certain angles, like a mini-mountain, giving the impression of an extinct volcano. It isn't, though it is volcanic in origin, an eroded remnant of a vast chunk of rock thrust to the surface around 700 million years ago, putting it among the oldest rocks in the world.

Fact or Fiction

If that origin seems a bit mundane, you might prefer the alternative provided by local folklore, which tells of the giant Gwendol Wrekin ap Shenkin ap Mynyddmawr (or the Devil in another version) who was on his way to Shrewsbury to dam the River Severn with a shovelful of soil. He met a cobbler who guessed what he was up to, showed him the sackful of shoes he was carrying and told him he had worn them all out trying to find Shrewsbury. Frustrated, Gwendol dumped his shovelful on the spot, sparing Shrewsbury from flooding and creating The Wrekin. (It didn't work, however – Shrewsbury floods nearly every winter.)

Ancient Rock

The return leg of the walk takes you through The Ercall Nature Reserve. The Ercall (pronounced arkle) is a small, steep, wooded hill important for its geology as well as its woodlands and wildlife. It has been much quarried and the sheer quarry faces are exciting to explore. Much of The Ercall is composed of Wrekin quartzite, a hard, white, crystalline rock around 535 million years old. It also has what geologists call an intrusion of granophyre, a fine-grained granite formed 560 million years ago, and a source of china clay. The great civil engineer Thomas Telford (1757–1834) used Ercall granophyre when he resurfaced the Roman Watling Street to create his much admired Holyhead Road, on which the modern A5 is based. Do stop to read the information boards in the nature reserve if you would like to know more about the geology and ecology of The Ercall, which is managed by Shropshire Wildlife Trust in partnership with Telford and Wrekin Council.

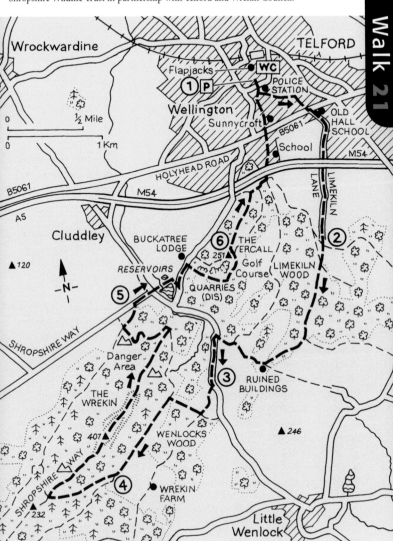

Walk 21 Directions

① Walk along **Tan Bank** away from the town centre. Cross **Victoria Road** and go forward a little way, still on Tan Bank, before turning left on a path just after the police

station. Walk to **New Church Road** and turn right. At **Holyhead Road**, turn left, then cross to **Limekiln Lane**, noticing the Old Hall School (built in 1480) on the corner. Soon the slopes of The Wrekin appear, as Limekiln Lane heads under the M54 into open country.

Walk 21

② At the end of the lane, go straight on into **Limekiln Wood**; the path leads along the edge of the wood at first. When you reach a junction, go to the left, but a few paces further on fork right into the heart of the wood. Ignore any branching paths, sticking to the well-trodden main route. Arriving at a T-junction by some ruined buildings, turn right, descend to a junction and turn left, then left

> **WHAT TO LOOK FOR** ⓘ
> **Limekiln Wood** is full of intriguing humps and hollows, overgrown now by ferns and ivy but still hinting at its former role as a quarry. Coal and limestone were dug here and much of the limestone was burnt on site in kilns, two of which survive (they're not on the route of this walk). The resulting lime was used in agriculture and building.

again when you come to a road.

③ Turn right on the access road to **Wrekin Farm**. When you reach **Wenlocks Wood**, leave the farm road, turning right on a field-edge footpath which heads towards The Wrekin. A stile soon gives access to its eastern slopes. Go forward a few paces, then turn left.

④ Branch right where a signpost indicates a permissive path. Follow

> **WHERE TO EAT AND DRINK** ⓘ
> The **Dun Cow** on Duke Street and the **White Lion** on Crown Street in Wellington are traditional pubs. **Café del Manso** next to the bus station has outside tables, very pleasant on sunny days. But my vote goes to **Flapjacks**, a friendly tea room and restaurant on Bell Street at the end of Tan Bank. No dogs allowed, unfortunately, but children are welcome and there is a reasonable veggie selection.

> **WHILE YOU'RE THERE** ⓘ
> Why not visit one of the National Trust's more unusual properties? You'll pass close by it when you cross Holyhead Road towards the end of the walk. A Victorian suburban house called **Sunnycroft**, it is typical of many built for prosperous professionals and businessmen, and has survived largely unaltered, its original contents still in place. The garden has pigsties, stables, orchards and even a wellingtonia avenue.

this round the hill to a cross path; turn right, joining the **Shropshire Way** for the climb over the summit ridge. As you approach the northern end, keep left when the path forks, then left again by a prominent beech tree, descending through woods. At the edge of the woods, leave the Shropshire Way and turn right to meet a lane.

⑤ Turn right to a T-junction, join a footpath opposite and pass between two reservoirs before meeting a lane, where you go left. As you draw almost level with **Buckatree Lodge**, turn right into **The Ercall Nature Reserve**. Go straight on along a bridleway, past some impressive former quarries and a pool. Before long you come to a junction; ignore a path doubling back towards the quarries and go forward a few paces to find that the main track swings left and climbs to the top of **The Ercall**.

⑥ As Wellington comes briefly into view through the trees, turn right on a ridge-top path. As you begin to descend, the path forks. Go to the right and shortly join a track which passes under the **M54**. Keep straight on along **Golf Links Lane** to **Holyhead Road**. Cross to a footpath opposite. When you reach a road (**Roseway**) turn right, then left on

Along the Staffordshire & Worcestershire Canal

An easy, family walk following the canal and a section of the disused Kingswinford railway track.

•DISTANCE•	4½ miles (7.2km)
•MINIMUM TIME•	1hr 30min
•ASCENT / GRADIENT•	59ft (18m)
•LEVEL OF DIFFICULTY•	
•PATHS•	Canal tow path, disused railway track and field paths, 1 stile
•LANDSCAPE•	Open countryside near urban residences
•SUGGESTED MAP•	aqua3 OS Explorer 219 Wolverhampton & Dudley
•START / FINISH•	Grid reference: SP 870982
•DOG FRIENDLINESS•	Off lead along tow path and disused railway, otherwise under control
•PARKING•	Near Mermaid pub, Wightwick
•PUBLIC TOILETS•	None on route

BACKGROUND TO THE WALK

This is a journey into the 18th and 19th centuries; a time when the canals and railways preceded our modern, noisy road network. The walk follows the tow path of the Staffordshire and Worcestershire Canal and a stretch of disused railway line to Compton. Nearby Wightwick (pronounced 'Wittick') Manor is easy to visit along the route (see While You're There).

Canal Revolution

If a contest for the Greatest Briton had taken place at the end of the 19th century, one of the main contenders would surely have been James Brindley. He helped to revolutionise Britain's transport system by building a series of remarkable canals that linked virtually all of the major cities in the country. The Staffordshire and Worcestershire Canal was one of his early constructions, built to link the Severn at Stourport with the Trent at Great Heywood and carry coal from the Staffordshire coalfields. Brindley's waterways were built on the contour principle, following the lie of the land. This approach avoided straight lines of canal, deep cuttings, massive embankments and large groups of lock gates. Work on the Staffordshire and Worcestershire Canal began in 1766 and was eventually completed in 1772. When you walk along the tow path you can imagine the dirty barges of the late 18th and early 19th centuries being hauled along by horses, accompanied by inquisitive children, dogs and local people. Commercial traffic finally ceased on the canal in 1960 and in 1978 the whole canal, including its buildings and its signs, was designated a conservation area.

As the Industrial Revolution progressed, canal barges were effectively replaced by steam trains, but there were gaps in the rail network. The Kingswinford branch was built by the Great Western Railway to fill one of these, allowing through traffic from Bridgnorth to Wolverhampton. It opened in 1925 but was never a great success for passengers. It became a freight only line in 1932, carrying people again briefly during World War Two, when it was

Walk 22

used to transfer wounded soldiers from the Normandy landings. The last train ran in 1965. The lines were dismantled and the Kingswinford Railway Walk was introduced to allow local people to use the former line for leisure purposes. When you walk along the now disused railway, try to visualise youngsters peering over the railway bridges through a cloud of smoke to get a glimpse of the mighty trains as they chuffed their way along the cutting.

Today the canal is used by pleasure boats and its tow path combines with the disused railway to provide a fine urban walk away from the noise of the busy road traffic.

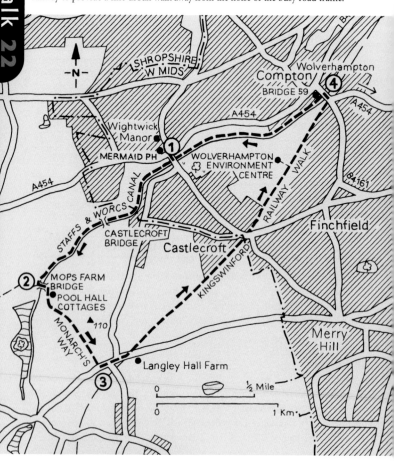

Walk 22 Directions

① From the car park, cross the **A454** at the pedestrian crossing to enter **Windmill Lane**. Bear right and descend to the tow path of the **Staffordshire and Worcestershire Canal**, heading in a south-westerly direction. Initially the tow path leads along the back of private

residences. After passing the **Cee-Ders Club** (on the far side of the canal), you reach open countryside, with ducks, coots and moorhens for company. This stretch of the canal is similar to a river and you are likely to see anglers fishing for perch, roach, chub, bream or carp. You may even see a colourful narrowboat pass by. Continue beneath bridge No 55 (**Castlecroft**

Bridge) and along the tow path until you come to bridge No 54 (**Mops Farm Bridge**).

② Leave the tow path and cross the bridge. Go right past **Pool Hall Cottages** and follow the the waymarkers of the Monarch's Way, heading generally south east. At first the path is to the right of the field hedge then, later, it crosses over to the left-hand side until you come to a stile to reach **Langley Road**.

> **WHAT TO LOOK FOR** ⓘ
> You may not see a horse-drawn coal barge as you stroll the tow path of the 46-mile (74km) long Staffordshire and Worcestershire Canal, but you are likely to meet a colourful **narrowboat** making its way through one of the lock gates. Pause a while and watch how it is lifted or dropped to another level. Compton Lock, just beyond Compton village, was the first lock to be built on this canal.

③ Go left up the road to the junction, then bear right through a small gateway to descend to the dismantled railway. Head left and follow the Kingswinford (South Staffordshire) Railway Walk. This is easy walking and you are likely to meet a number of other walkers and possibly cyclists. Continue for about 2 miles (3.2km). You will eventually pass beneath the road bridge near **Castlecroft**; following this there are moments when the scene opens up. After passing the **Wolverhampton Environment Centre** you come to **Compton**.

> **WHERE TO EAT AND DRINK** ⓘ
> Eating out in the small front garden of the **Mermaid** watching the world go by is the perfect way to end a perfect day. Children are also welcome. If you visit Wightwick Manor, you can enjoy a quiet leisurely lunch in the **Tea Room** on Wednesdays, Thursdays and bank holidays. Alternatively, you can get good food at **Bridge 59 restaurant** (Point ④) or the **Milestone** in Compton.

Leave the disused railway line and climb up to the **A454**, going left.

④ Go left again and descend by the side of the **Bridge No 59 restaurant** on to the tow path and take it back to **bridge No 56**, passing a couple of lock gates and a number of moored narrowboats. Go beneath bridge No 56 and leave the canal on to the pavement of **Windmill Lane**. Continue towards the main **A454** road and cross over to return to the **Mermaid** in Wightwick.

> **WHILE YOU'RE THERE** ⓘ
> Nearby **Wightwick Manor** was built in 1887 by the Mander family. This half-timbered building is now owned and maintained by the National Trust. The influence of the 19th-century decorative artist William Morris is clear to see. Original Morris wallpapers, Pre-Raphaelite pictures, stained glass by C E Kempe and De Morgan tiles are on display. There are also fine gardens laid out with terraces and pools and some splendid yew hedges and topiary.

Kinver's Impressive Rock Houses

A short walk combining curious cave dwellings with some of the best views in Staffordshire.

•DISTANCE•	2¾ miles (4.4km)
•MINIMUM TIME•	1hr
•ASCENT / GRADIENT•	374ft (114m) ▲▲▲
•LEVEL OF DIFFICULTY•	
•PATHS•	Wide gravel tracks
•LANDSCAPE•	Woodland and escarpment top
•SUGGESTED MAP•	aqua3 OS Explorer 219 Wolverhampton & Dudley
•START / FINISH•	Grid reference: SJ 835836
•DOG FRIENDLINESS•	Can be taken off lead
•PARKING•	Ample parking in car park at start
•PUBLIC TOILETS•	None on route

BACKGROUND TO THE WALK

The impressive sandstone ridge to the south west of Kinver has been occupied in one way or another since 2500 BC, and impressive earthworks, believed to have been built at around this time, still exist near the summit.

Kinver Edge

The views from the summit, and in fact along the length of Kinver Edge, are indeed tremendous, and it must have seemed an impressive vantage point on which to build defences. Today, a brass relief map at the north end (Point ②), presented by the local Rotary Club in 1990, points to a selection of the world's major capitals, in addition to less distant landmarks. Both the Malvern Hills, 30 miles (48km) to the south, and Long Mynd, the same distance to the west, are visible on a clear day and, at times, it may be possible to see the Black Mountains, over 45 miles (72km) away. But for all its breathtaking views, the real interest on Kinver Edge lies below the summit, in small houses carved into the rock.

Holy Austin Rock

Of these, by far the most impressive are the dwellings at Holy Austin Rock, a short walk to the east of the car park. Legend has it that it was named after a hermit who lived near the site. The first written reference to people actually living in houses cut out of the rock face is believed to be in a book about a walk in the area, written in 1777. The author, seeking shelter from a storm, encounters 'this exceedingly curious rock inhabited by a clean and decent family', before going on to describe the rooms as 'really curious warm and commodious'.

Family Homes

By the beginning of the 19th century there were several rock houses, and for the next 100 years or so they were permanently occupied. By 1861 there were 11 families in residence, the increase almost certainly due to the demand created by the local iron works. When these went into decline at the end of the 19th century, the houses were gradually abandoned. Having said that, two families continued to live there until the end of World War Two, and the last occupants didn't move out until 1963. A tourist café also lasted until 1967, after which the houses suffered decades of decline and neglect: vandalism led to collapses and, sadly, one area had to be destroyed for safety reasons.

Postcard Plans

It wasn't until the 1980s that plans were finally drawn up to renovate the houses to their original state, a task which was achieved with the help of postcards popular 100 years earlier. The rebuilding was completed in 1993 and the site was again occupied, this time by a National Trust custodian. While this house is private, the rest of the site is open to the public all year round. The lower rock houses are only open on weekend afternoons between March the end of November (2–4pm).

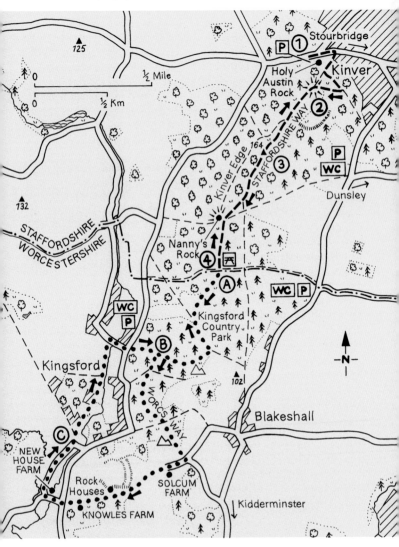

Visitors can see how occupants would have lived 100 or so years ago, and may be surprised at just how cosy the houses feel. The combination of thick sandstone and fireplaces would have kept them warm in winter and cool in summer, whilst in many places interior walls were plastered and whitewashed. Today, Holy Austin Rock has also been designated as a Site of Special Scientific Interest (SSSI) for its sandstone, which was formed from solidified sand dunes in the Permian era, 250 million years ago.

Walk 23 Directions

① From the National Trust car park, head back along the road towards **Kinver** village. Within 100yds (91m), after going right at a fork in the road, follow public footpath signs to the right, up into the woods. Once you're in the woods proper, take the obvious stepped path left to the small clearing and then turn 90 degrees to the right to follow the short, steep path to the viewpoint.

② From the viewpoint, continue along the top of the escarpment, following a wide, gravel track running more or less alongside the western edge of the ancient rectangular earthworks to the left, with glimpsed views across the Severn Valley through trees to the right. After 400yds (366m) you come to the end of the clearing. Take the fork to your left here, up a slight rise at the corner of the earthworks, before carrying on along the escarpment top, past the **trig point**.

WHAT TO LOOK FOR

Nanny's Rock, just inside the National Trust boundary, and just off the path, provides a breathtaking viewpoint and a great place to sit and have a picnic or admire the view – it too has a collection of simple cave or rock dwellings carved out beneath, although considerable care should be taken to reach them as the ground is a bit steep and rocky.

③ Staying on the highest path, continue as far as the National Trust boundary gate and then continue straight along the main track avoiding smaller trails off to the left and right. The path descends gradually to a picnic spot with benches, an information board and signs for the Staffordshire Way and the Worcestershire Way. A narrow track to the right leads back down to the road and a public toilet if required, although it criss-crosses other paths and it's very easy to lose your bearings!

WHERE TO EAT AND DRINK

The **Vine Inn** has a beer garden right on the canal at Dunsley and is ideal for children and dogs in the summer, when it serves burgers, sandwiches and other bar snacks outdoors. The food is good value and the portions are suitably generous.

④ For this reason, it's easiest to return the way you came. From the path junction, head back along the escarpment to the viewpoint. At the end, head right and then left, back down to the clearing, and then left again down the wooden steps, through the trees to the road. Follow the road left as far as the car park. For those armed with the relevant OS map, there is a suitable alternative which returns via the forested slopes to the west of the ridge top, but because of the number of little tracks that cross back and forth, it's difficult to give adequate directions here.

Worcestershire Loop

Extend the walk to take in an ancient fort and some additional rock houses.
See map and information panel for Walk 23

•DISTANCE•	6 miles (9.7km)
•MINIMUM TIME•	2hrs
•ASCENT / GRADIENT•	750ft (229m) ▲▲▲
•LEVEL OF DIFFICULTY•	

Walk 24 Directions (Walk 23 option)

From Point Ⓐ, continue along the escarpment, following the **Worcestershire Way** (indicated by a small yellow arrow). When you get to a path junction (signed with lots of coloured arrows), continue along the Worcestershire Way. At the edge of the wood with three footpath options, head right into the trees and down a fairly steep path.

Where this path meets a gate and a more obvious sand track at right angles (Point Ⓑ), head left. After 300yds (274m) you come to another path junction. Take the smallest, central path, following the yellow arrow. On reaching a sandy track go straight over, coming shortly to a steep hill. When you get to the clearing at the top, cross the stile and continue in the same direction, with a fence to your left. In the far left corner of the field, cross another stile on to the metalled road.

Head right towards Solcum Farm, passing **Moat Court Farm** on the right and, shortly after, **Solcum Farm** on the left. Head to the right of Solcum Farm following a

succession of yellow arrows down a dark and heavily wooded track as far as **Knowles Farm**. At the crossroads continue straight on and take the first right at **New House Farm.** Carry on to where the surfaced road turns to the right and follow the track off left (Point Ⓒ).

Immediately after Point Ⓒ, take the right fork and, when the track turns left, continue straight on to the right of the fence, following the yellow arrows. Soon after crossing a stile, turn right along the metalled road until it meets a bigger road. Go straight across and up a footpath just to the left, signed 'Blakeshall'. When this path meets a wide sand bridleway (Point Ⓑ again), continue across and back up the way you came, retracing your steps back to the picnic site.

WHAT TO LOOK FOR ⓘ

As you descend into the dark woods beyond Solcum Farm, the steep bank to the right forms the remains of some **Iron-Age earthworks** not unlike the one at the start of the walk. Just before you get to the derelict buildings of Knowles Farm, turn right off the main path up a dirt track to reach another group of **rock houses**. These are far less developed than those at Kinver, which makes them all the more appealing, as it's possible to wander into different rooms.

The Wood Colliers' Legacy at Clunton

A leafy walk from Clunton Coppice to Purslow Wood.

•DISTANCE•	3¾ miles (6km)
•MINIMUM TIME•	1hr 15min
•ASCENT / GRADIENT•	574ft (17m) ▲ ▲ ▲
•LEVEL OF DIFFICULTY•	
•PATHS•	Woodland paths, grassy track, quiet lanes and Forestry Commission paths, some overgrown, no stiles
•LANDSCAPE•	Woodland and plantation on steep valley sides
•SUGGESTED MAP•	aqua3 OS Explorer 201 Knighton & Presteigne
•START / FINISH•	Grid reference: SO 338805
•DOG FRIENDLINESS•	Great walk for dogs
•PARKING•	Small car park near nature reserve sign at Clunton Coppice on Cwm Lane, which runs south from Clunton
•PUBLIC TOILETS•	None on route

Walk 25 Directions

Half a century ago the dominant woodland type in south west Shropshire was sessile oak. Not much remains today, so it's fortunate that one of the largest surviving woods, Clunton Coppice, is owned by Shropshire Wildlife Trust. In the distant past it was managed for charcoal production, which involved coppicing. This is a

system of woodland management in which trees are cut close to the ground, then left to grow again. The cut stools quickly put out new shoots which can be harvested for small timber or left to grow on. Where coppicing is still carried out it is usually for wildlife rather than commercial purposes.

Leaving the car park, carry on along the lane until a footpath leaves it on the left. Follow it through **Clunton Coppice**, noticing the variety of species. Sessile oak is dominant, but small-leaved lime, yew and hornbeam also occur, while the shrub layer includes hazel, holly and rowan. Some hazel or oak is coppiced every year and the brash (the stuff too small to be used as firewood) is piled on the slow-growing oak stools to prevent deer nibbling the tender regrowth. The charcoal burners (or wood colliers, as they were often known in the Marches) who worked Clunton

---

WHILE YOU'RE THERE ⓘ

Shropshire Wildlife Trust has 37 reserves altogether and welcomes the public to almost all of them. Why not visit the Trust's centre on Abbey Foregate in Shrewsbury? The centre itself is a nature reserve, with many birds breeding in the garden, which is a re-creation of a medieval physic garden. The Trust inherited this when it took up residence in 2001 and intends to save the most interesting plants, while also making it a true wildlife garden.

Walk 25

Coppice in the past would have lived in the wood all summer, sleeping under simple shelters, because it was important to keep the charcoal kilns continuously alight and closely regulated to avoid flare-ups.

WHAT TO LOOK FOR

Damp oak woods are good places to find **non-flowering plants** such as mosses, ferns and fungi. Clunton Coppice is no exception and the luxuriant growth of vivid green mosses is one of its most attractive attributes. Ferns and fungi are plentiful too, but can you find *Phellinus robustus*, a bracket fungus which lives high up in the branches? This is so scarce that it has been recorded in only two British locations – Windsor Great Park and Clunton Coppice.

The path becomes a track, which descends past **Badgers Croft** to a lane. Continue straight on for about 50yds (46m) until you've passed **The Meadows**. Go through a gate on the right into a field and diagonally left up the slope into **Purslow Wood**, a Forestry Commission plantation. Follow a track uphill, soon emerging from the trees into a felled area. Keep climbing, shortly crossing a forestry track. Pick the best way up through scrub, dodging fallen trees and brash (you can avoid this if you wish by staying on the track, turning right, then left) to rejoin the forestry track. Turn left, climb to a junction and go left for a few

paces. Leave the forestry track, going across a turning area to join a bridleway that climbs slightly. When a fence blocks your way, turn left to rejoin the forestry track.

Turn right for 20yds (18m), then go downhill on a bridleway, which is overgrown with bracken and bramble. Turn left when you meet a lane. If you prefer to avoid the overgrown bridleway you can do so by continuing along the forestry track for a further 350yds (320m), then turning sharp left on a path which descends to the lane. Bear in mind that it's only by actually using overgrown paths that we can most easily keep these routes open.

Follow the lane back to the point at which you met it earlier, when descending from Clunton Coppice. Instead of returning up the track the same way, join a green lane which starts just before a field gate. Follow it past a house and garden, then along the northern edge of Clunton Coppice and ultimately past **Bush Farm**, where it becomes a paved lane leading to a junction on the edge of **Clunton**. Turn left up **Cwm Lane** to return to **Clunton Coppice**. Just as you reach the coppice, look for a group of hornbeam trees on the left. Hornbeam is superficially a little like beech, but is distinguished from it by its smooth fluted trunk and winged fruits. It's an uncommon tree this far north.

WHERE TO EAT AND DRINK

In 1994 the **Crown Inn** at Clunton was threatened with closure, like so many country pubs. However, the locals knew just how to save it. They clubbed together and bought it, and happily it is still going strong today. The present couple running it took over in 2002 and are keen to attract more walkers, so you can be sure of a warm welcome, and not just from the woodburning stove. Food is served from noon, children and well-behaved dogs are welcome (dogs on leads), and the landlord specifically points out that walkers do not have to remove their boots.

Romancing the Stones in the Preseli Hills

Easy walking to a spectacular hill around some of the most mystical rocks on the planet.

•DISTANCE•	5½ miles (8.8km)
•MINIMUM TIME•	2hrs 30min
•ASCENT / GRADIENT•	560ft (170m) ▲▲▲
•LEVEL OF DIFFICULTY•	
•PATHS•	Mainly clear paths across open moorland, no stiles
•LANDSCAPE•	Rolling hills topped with rocky outcrops
•SUGGESTED MAP•	aqua3 OS Explorer OL35 North Pembrokeshire
•START / FINISH•	Grid reference: SO 165331
•DOG FRIENDLINESS•	Care needed near livestock
•PARKING•	Small lay-by on lane beneath Foeldrygarn
•PUBLIC TOILETS•	None on route but plenty of sheltered nooks and crannies
•NOTE•	Navigation very difficult in poor visibility

BACKGROUND TO THE WALK

A circular walk around the most interesting sites of the Preseli Hills is almost impossible. The uplands form an isolated east–west ridge that would at best form one side of a circuit linked with a lengthy road section. Instead of taking this less-than-ideal option, this walk forms a contorted and narrow figure-of-eight that scales the most spectacular hill on the ridge, traces the line of the famous dolerite outcrops, or carns, and then makes an out-and-back sortie to an impressive stone circle. Convoluted it may be, but it's packed with interest and easy going enough for most people to complete comfortably.

Preseli Hills

The Pembrokeshire Coast National Park is best known for its stunning coastline. Britain's smallest National Park is in no single place further than 10 miles (16.1km) from the sea. This furthest point was a deliberate extension of the boundaries to incorporate one of the most important historic sites in the United Kingdom, the Preseli Hills.

Carn Menyn's Bluestones

It was from Carn Menyn, one of the rocky tors that crown the marshy and often windswept hills, that the bluestones forming the inner circle of Stonehenge were taken. These bluestones, or spotted dolerite stones to give them their proper name, would have each weighed somewhere in the region of 4 tons and must have been transported over 200 miles (320km) in total. To this day we cannot explain how or why.

Ancient Road

The Stonehenge story, significant as it may be, is only part of the historic and, at times, mystical feel of this narrow, grassy upland. The track that follows the ridge is an ancient road, perhaps dating back over 5,000 years. It's probable that it was a safe passage between the coast and the settlements inland at a time when wild predators such as bears and wolves roamed the valleys below. Gravestones line the track, most likely those of travellers or traders who were buried where they died, and other standing stones dot the hillsides.

Beddarthur

West of Carn Menyn, beneath another impressive outcrop named Carn Bica, there's a stone circle known as Beddarthur. Small by comparison to Stonehenge or Avebury, its oval arrangement of 2ft–3ft (0.6m–1m) high stones is said to be yet another burial place of King Arthur; 'bedd' means grave in Welsh. There are certainly links between the legendary historical superhero and the area; it's suggested that the King and his knights chased Twrch Trywyth, the magical giant boar, across these hills before heading east.

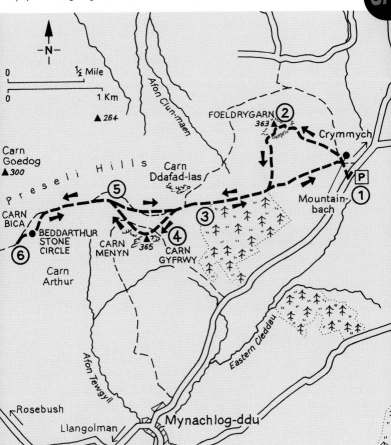

Walk 26 Directions

① Walk to the right out of the lay-by on the lane from Crymych, then turn right up a stony track. When you reach the gate, keep going straight ahead for another 100yds (91m) or so, and then fork left on to a grassy track, which soon becomes clearer as it winds its way up the hillside. Follow this all the way to the rocky cairns and trig point on **Foeldrygarn**.

Walk 26

② Bear left at the summit and locate a grassy track that drops to the south. Cross the heather-clad plateau beneath, aiming for the left-hand corner of a wood. When you meet the main track, turn right to walk with the edge of the wood on your left.

③ Leaving the wood, the path climbs slightly to some rocky tors. The second of these, the one that's closest to the track, has a sheepfold at its base. Shortly after this, the path forks and you follow the left-hand track down to the nearest of the group of outcrops to your left.

④ This is **Carn Gyfrwy**. Continue on faint paths to the larger outcrops ahead, then curve right and drop slightly to **Carn Menyn**, the lowest of the bunch, perched precariously on the edge of the escarpment. The path becomes clearer here and drops slightly into a marshy saddle

that can be seen ahead.

⑤ In the saddle you'll meet the main track. Turn left and follow it steadily up towards **Carn Bica**, which is visible on the hillside ahead of you. Just before this, you'll cross the circle made by the stones of **Beddarthur**.

⑥ Turn around and retrace your steps back to the saddle. Climb slightly to pass the tor with the sheepfold and stay on this main path to walk beside the plantation once more, now on your right. At the end of this, drop, on a grassy track, down to the gate. Turn right on to the lane and continue back to

Woodland and Family Wars at Oxwich Point

A short but very exhilarating ramble through woodland and along delightful coastline.

Walk 27

•DISTANCE•	4½ miles (7.2km)
•MINIMUM TIME•	2hrs
•ASCENT / GRADIENT•	480ft (146m) ▲▲▲
•LEVEL OF DIFFICULTY•	
•PATHS•	Clear paths through woodland, along coast and across farmland, quiet lane, 6 stiles
•LANDSCAPE•	Mixed woodland and rugged coastline
•SUGGESTED MAP•	aqua3 OS Explorer 164 Gower
•START / FINISH•	Grid reference: SS 500864
•DOG FRIENDLINESS•	Can mostly run free
•PARKING•	Oxwich Bay
•PUBLIC TOILETS•	At car park near start

BACKGROUND TO THE WALK

The Gower has less obvious headlands than nearby Pembrokeshire and this makes it much more difficult to fashion short but interesting circular walks. This one stands out for a couple of reasons. Firstly, it can be combined with a visit to Oxwich National Nature Reserve, a treasure trove of marshland and sand dunes in a wonderful beachside location. Secondly, the wonderful coastal scenery includes the beautiful and usually deserted beach known as The Sands. And finally, being short, it allows plenty of time for exploring both the atmospheric St Illtud's Church and the majestic ruins of Oxwich Castle.

Oxwich Village
Once a busy port that paid its way by shipping limestone from quarries on the rugged headland, Oxwich is now one of the prettiest and most unspoilt Gower villages, due in no small part to its distance from the main roads. The name is derived from Axwick, Norse for Water Creek. For maximum enjoyment, it's best visited away from the main holiday seasons.

St Illtud's
Founded in the 6th century AD and tucked away in a leafy clearing above the beach, St Illtud's Church is particularly significant for its stone font, which is said to have been donated by St Illtud himself. The grounds are tranquil with an atmosphere that comes in stark contrast to the summertime chaos of the beach below. Behind the building is the grave of an unknown soldier who was washed up on the beach during World War Two. It's certainly a spooky spot and the graveyard is purported to be haunted by a strange half-man-half-horse creature.

St Illtud (or St Illtyd) was a Welsh-born monk who founded the nearby abbey of Llan-Illtut (Llantwit Major). He is perhaps most famous for his fights against famine which included sailing grain ships to Brittany. He died in Brittany in AD 505.

Walk 27

Feuding Families

Really a 16th-century mansion house built by Sir Rhys Mansel on the site of the 14th-century castle, Oxwich Castle occupies an airy setting above the bay. Sir Rhys, in common with many Gower locals, wasn't above plundering the cargo of ships that came to grief in the bay and was quick to take advantage of a French wreck in late December 1557. The salvage rights, however, belonged to a Sir George Herbert of Swansea, who quickly paid Mansel a visit to reclaim his goods. A fight broke out and Sir Rhys's daughter Anne was injured by a stone thrown by Herbert's servant. She later died from her injuries. Court action against Herbert proved ineffective and there followed a feud which continued for many years until eventually the Mansel family moved to Margam, east of Swansea. Part of the mansion was leased to local farmers, but most of the fine building fell into disrepair.

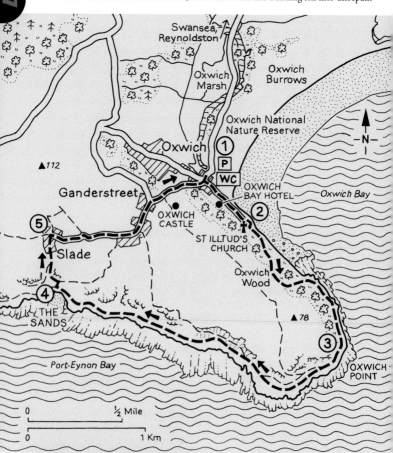

Walk 27 Directions

① Walk back out of the car park and turn left to a crossroads. Turn left here (waymarked 'Eglwys') and pass the **Woodside Guesthouse** and the **Oxwich Bay Hotel**, on your right. This lane leads into the woods and up to 6th-century **St Illtud's Church**, where a gate marks the end of the road and the start of a path leading out on to Oxwich Point.

② Go through the gate and bear right, going up the wooden steps to climb steeply up through the wood. As the footpath levels, bear left to drop back down through the wood and around the headland until it comes out into the open above **Oxwich Point**.

③ The path drops through gorse and bracken to become a grassy coast path that runs easily above a rocky beach. Keep the sea on your left and ignore any tracks that run off to the right. After approximately 1 mile (1.6km) you'll pass a distinct valley that drops in from your right. Continue past this and cross a succession of stiles, until you reach the sandy beach of **The Sands**.

④ Turn right, behind the beach, and follow a narrow footpath to a stile. This leads on to a broad farm track, where you turn left. Continue up and around to the right until you come to a galvanised kissing gate. Go through this and keep right to head up a lane past some houses to a crossroads.

Walk 27

⑤ Turn right here and follow the road along to a fork where you keep right. Drop down to the entrance of **Oxwich Castle** on the right. After looking at or exploring the castle, turn right, back on to the lane, and head down into **Oxwich** village. Keep straight ahead to the car park.

Walk 28

Moel Famau: the Mother Mountain

Walk to the highest of the Clwydian Hills and see a beautiful wooded limestone valley on the way.

•DISTANCE•	8 miles (12.9km)
•MINIMUM TIME•	5hrs
•ASCENT / GRADIENT•	1,608ft (490m) ▲▲▲
•LEVEL OF DIFFICULTY•	
•PATHS•	Well-defined paths and forestry tracks, 9 stiles
•LANDSCAPE•	Heather moor, forest and farmland
•SUGGESTED MAP•	aqua3 OS Explorer 265 Clwydian Range
•START / FINISH•	Grid reference: SJ 198625
•DOG FRIENDLINESS•	Dogs could run free in forest and on heather ridges
•PARKING•	Pay car park by Loggerheads Country Park Visitor Centre
•PUBLIC TOILETS•	At Visitor Centre
•NOTE•	Route can be shortened by taking regular Moel Famau shuttle bus, which runs on Sundays (July to September) and bank holidays, from forestry car park to Loggerheads.

BACKGROUND TO THE WALK

If you're driving into Wales from the north west, the chances are that the first hills you'll see are the Clwydians, dark rolling ridges that rise up from the sea at Prestatyn and decline 20 miles (32km) or so south in the fields of the Alun Valley. Although the hills are empty these days, at one time they were highly populated. Climb to the tops and you'll see Iron- and Bronze-Age forts scattered about the hilltops, some of them among the best preserved in Wales.

At Loggerheads

One of the best places to start a walk in the Clwydians is Loggerheads. The path from the information centre follows the shallow but swift-flowing River Alun through a narrow limestone valley filled with wych elm and oak. In July, you'll see excellent limestone flora, including field scabious, wild thyme, rock rose and bloody cranesbill, while in the trees there are spotted woodpeckers, tawny owls and nuthatches.

On the Top

The climb out of the valley includes a short traverse of farmland before clambering through heather fields to Moel Famau, which means 'mother mountain' and at 1,818ft (554m) is the highest of the range. The monument on the summit was built in 1810 to celebrate the jubilee of King George III. Its square tower and spire were wrecked by a violent gale 50 years later, and the place lay in ruins until 1970 when it was tidied up. Below and to the west there's the much older site of Moel y Gaer, one of those fascinating hill forts with concentric earthwork rings sculpted into a grassy knoll. Casting your eyes beyond the rings and across the green fields and chequered hedgerows of the Vale of Clwyd, it's fascinating to pick out the familiar skyline summits of Snowdonia. Tryfan's jagged crest is easy to spot, but somehow you cannot quite see Snowdon: that's because Moel Siabod, prima donna that it feels it is, has elbowed its way to the front, to hide the real star, Snowdon, and confuse the issue. Fortunately there are topographs to help you out.

The ridge walking from the summit is delightful, and on a good day you might wish to extend your day by doing the Walk 29 extension. Otherwise, a wide path takes you down to the forest, where it continues down a grassy ride. While the spruce trees are not an attractive habitat for a wide range of species you might easily spot a song thrush, colourful chaffinches or coal tits; or maybe, just maybe, a sparrowhawk. Country lanes and farm pastures take you down to the banks of the River Alun which guides you back to Loggerheads.

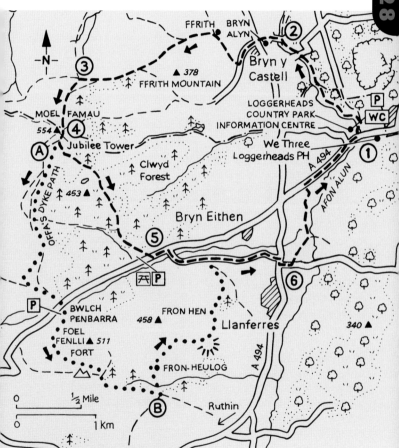

Walk 28 Directions

① Go past the front of the **Loggerheads Country Park Information Centre**, cross the bridge over the Alun and turn left along the surfaced path through the valley. Where the path splits, follow the route on the left, marked the **Leete Path**.

② Look out for a small and slippery-when-wet path on the left beyond the **Alyn Kennels**. This takes you down to a footbridge

Walk 28

across the river. Across this the path heads west, then staggers to the right across a farm lane and climbs past a farmhouse. Enclosed by thickets, it climbs to the right of **Bryn Alyn** (cottage) to reach a T-junction of country lanes. Go straight ahead and follow the lane uphill, then turn right to follow the track that passes **Ffrith farm** before swinging left to climb round the pastured slopes of **Ffrith Mountain**. Take the left fork in the tracks (at grid ref 177637).

WHILE YOU'RE THERE ⓘ

You could pay to go to prison. **Ruthin's Old Gaol**, built in 1654, is described as 'the Gruelling Experience' and opened its heavy doors in May 2002. The Gaoler and Will the Poacher will guide you round the cells, including the punishment cells. They will tell you stories about the Welsh Houdini and William Hughes, who was the last person to be hanged here.

---

③ The route skirts a spruce plantation and climbs to a crossroads of tracks, marked by a tall waymarker post. Turn left here on a wide path over undulating heather slopes towards the tower on the top of **Moel Famau**.

④ From the summit, head south east and go over the stile at the end of the wall to follow a wide track, marked with red-tipped waymarker posts, south east along the forest's edge. The track continues its descent through the trees to meet the roadside car park/picnic area ¾ mile (1.2km) east of Bwlch Penbarra's summit (see Information Panel on using shuttle bus).

⑤ Turn left along the road, before turning right when you get to the first junction.

WHERE TO EAT AND DRINK ⓘ

The weirdly named **We Three Loggerheads**, opposite the country park, is an old pub serving Bass and Worthington beers and tasty bar meals.

The quiet lane leads to the busy **A494**. Cross the main road with care and continue along the hedge-lined lane staggered to the right.

⑥ A waymarked path on the left heads north east across fields towards the banks of the **Alun**. Don't cross the river at the bridge, but head north, through the gateway and across more fields, keeping to the right and above a substantial stone-built house to meet the **A494**. It's just ½ mile (800m) from here to the **Loggerheads Country Park** entrance, and there are verges and paths to walk on.

WHAT TO LOOK FOR ⓘ

You'll have seen the red grouse on many a British moor, but here there's a chance to see the rarer **black grouse**, a darker bird with a call more like a *tchack* than the *go-back, go-back* of the red grouse. In February the males put on a spectacular breeding dance, fanning their tails to show their white plumage beneath their wings and on their rump. They will also be hissing and crowing, quite oblivious to their surroundings and impending danger.

The Clwydian Skyline

A walk along the heather-clad ridges of the Clwydian Range.
See map and information panel for Walk 28

•**DISTANCE**•	10 miles (16.1km)
•**MINIMUM TIME**•	6hrs
•**ASCENT / GRADIENT**•	1,805ft (550m) ▲▲▲
•**LEVEL OF DIFFICULTY**•	◣

Walk 29 Directions (Walk 28 option)

Like Walk 28, this route takes you to the top of Moel Famau, but this time you stay high and walk south along the ridges that have been designated an Area of Outstanding Natural Beauty (AONB).

From Point ④, ignore the numerous tracks that descend from the summit to the forest, but instead stay with the wide path, that heads south along an undulating ridge, Point Ⓐ, with spruce woods to the left and gorse bushes and the odd hawthorn tree scattered amongst the heather and patches of bracken and bilberry. Look for the coloured Emperor moth. The male can often be seen fluttering fast and low over the heather, the female only comes out at dusk.

The wide track eventually descends to a high roadside car park at **Bwlch Penbarra**, where you'll often see a refreshment van. The route can be shortened by taking the regular Moel Famau shuttle bus, which runs on Sundays and bank holidays, July to September, from here back to Loggerheads. Across the road and the car park you can go on a direct path to the top of **Foel Fenlli**, the next hill, where you can see the earthwork remains of an Iron-Age fort. The best route, however, follows the **Offa's Dyke Path** around the west and south sides of the hill, passing through more heather and lush bilberry to reach the hill's high shoulder, alongside the outer rings of the large ancient fort.

The path descends steeply to a small plantation, before climbing beside its western edge. An Offa's Dyke waymark highlights our path which turns left by a fence to trace the edge of another plantation.

You come to a gate and a crossroads of paths, Point Ⓑ, south of **Fron-heulog farm**, which can be seen on the pastured hillside to the left. Turn left through the gate and follow the winding track to the top gate just to the left of the farm. Beyond this, swing right on a sunken track that climbs above the farm and offers superb views of the Alun Valley and the tiered limestone hills beyond.

The path follows the intake wall on the right, and arcs round the hillside of **Fron Hen**, coming out on a narrow country lane, where you turn right and rejoin Walk 28.

Gold in the King's Forest

Deep in Coed y Brenin you'll find two waterfalls and maybe a glint of gold.

•DISTANCE•	4 miles (6.4km)
•MINIMUM TIME•	2hrs
•ASCENT / GRADIENT•	656ft (200m) ▲▲▲
•LEVEL OF DIFFICULTY•	
•PATHS•	Forest tracks and paths, 2 stiles
•LANDSCAPE•	Forest
•SUGGESTED MAP•	aqua3 OS Explorer OL18 Harlech, Porthmadog & Bala
•START / FINISH•	Grid reference: SH 735263
•DOG FRIENDLINESS•	Dogs are okay in forest
•PARKING•	Tyddyn Gwladys forest car park near Ganllwyd
•PUBLIC TOILETS•	None on route

Walk 30 Directions

If ever there's a case for walking in the rain this is it. There are trees for shelter, two bounding rivers and two waterfalls which look their best when in spate. We'll settle for that as long as there's a dry spell when we reach the top of the small hill at the end of the valley.

The two rivers are the Mawddach, a great river that flows out to sea at Barmouth, and its tributary, the Gain. The trees are those of Coed y Brenin – the King's Forest.

Gold has been mined throughout Wales for centuries and there were large finds of good quality gold in the mid-19th century, when Dolgellau became another Klondyke. The rush was on. Morgan Pritchard owned the mining rights to the Mawddach and Cain areas and he started the gold mines at Gwynfynydd. Though hopes were high, the mine didn't really produce profitable lodes and work all but stopped in 1914, with only sporadic re-openings to produce rings for royal weddings. Today you'll see the odd prospector panning for gold in the river.

Turn right out of the car park and follow the flinted forestry track, with the Afon Mawddach below right.

The trees nearest the river consist of sessile oak, ash, birch and alder, planted by the Vaughan's in the 19th century, when this was part of their huge Nannau Estate. It's a wonderful haven for wildlife. You'll have a chance of seeing the red squirrel, which has been forced out of so many other areas by its larger grey cousin. There's also a chance you'll see a heron come to fish. Another angler, though it will be harder to spot, is the otter. Brown

---

WHAT TO LOOK FOR ⓘ

The **Goshawk** is a regular visitor to the forest. It's a large hawk with slate grey to brown upper colouring with white underneath. Recognised in flight by its long tail and short, broad wings, it makes a chattering *ca-ca-ca* or *keck-keck* sound.

Walk 30

trout and minnows are numerous, and each year salmon and sea trout brave the rapids by swimming upriver to spawn.

> **WHILE YOU'RE THERE**
> If you're in the mood for another waterfall, there's an even better one, **Rhaeadr Ddu** on the opposite side of the A470 at Ganllwyd. It's just a short stroll and it's a place that has inspired artists like Gainsborough and Turner.

The track passes beneath the **Mostyn cottages**, originally built for workers from the mines. Just beyond them you'll come to the Ferndale complex, now holiday cottages, but once the workshops and blasting plant. Take the high track on the left above these.

The track swings right to cross the **Afon Gain**, close to its confluence with the Mawddach. On the other side, detour left along the rough path that takes a closer look at the waterfalls, known as **Pistyll y Cain**. The impressive cascades splash 148ft (45m) against dark rocks into a black pool below; all this in the shadow of thick woodland and, in late spring, embellished by the blooms of rhododendrons.

Return to the main track, where you turn left to the old mine's mill buildings. Years ago this would be a hive of activity, but it's a rather sad scene now, with graffiti, keep out signs and pipes going nowhere.

Just beyond the mill area you come to the second waterfalls, those of **Rhaeadr Mawddach**. Though they're not as gracefully shaped, high, nor in such pleasant surroundings as Pistyll y Cain, they're nevertheless torrential and impressive. An old stone packhorse bridge beyond them has recently suffered damage and a new footbridge has been added. Don't cross here but double back left on a path climbing through a plantation of spruce, pine and larch. Ignore the cycle route on the right, near the beginning of this path.

After winding up the hillside, the path comes to a junction. Ignore the signed footpath going straight ahead, but instead turn right on a track marked with a white-topped post (No 30). This soon becomes a grassy path that comes out of the forest at a small gate, and continues as an enclosed path through high pastures in an area that was once the main Gwynfynydd Mine. The track passes above the farmhouse of **Ty Mawr**, where it becomes a lane.

> **WHERE TO EAT AND DRINK**
> The **Halfway House** at Bont Ddu is an 18th-century free house with pine chapel pews for some of the seating. They serve a wide range of traditional meals.

You're high on the hillside now and there's a view over the treetops and across the meandering Mawddach to two shapely mountains, Rhobell Fawr and Dduallt.

Turn right on meeting a quiet lane and follow it almost to **Bedd y Coedwr Farm**. A footpath signpost points the way downhill on a field path to the left of birch woods. The path veers right through heather-strewn scrubland and becomes rough and overgrown in places, until it reaches an old mine track by the banks of the **Mawddach**.

Follow the track past the mine shafts to reach the outward route by **Rhaeadr Mawddach**. Retrace your footsteps to the car park.

Walk 31

Wolfscote Dale and a Railway Trail

Wolfscote Dale and Biggin Dale wind through the heart of the upland limestone country.

•DISTANCE•	7½ miles (12.1km)
•MINIMUM TIME•	5hrs
•ASCENT / GRADIENT•	557ft (170m) ▲▲▲
•LEVEL OF DIFFICULTY•	
•PATHS•	Generally well-defined paths, limestone dale sides can be slippery after rain, quite a few stiles
•LANDSCAPE•	Partially wooded limestone dales and high pasture
•SUGGESTED MAP•	aqua3 OS Explorer OL24 White Peak
•START / FINISH•	Grid reference: SK 156549
•DOG FRIENDLINESS•	Can run free on much of walk
•PARKING•	Tissington Trail pay car park (by Stonepit Plantation)
•PUBLIC TOILETS•	None on route

BACKGROUND TO THE WALK

From its source, on Axe Edge, to Hartington the River Dove is little more than a stream, flowing almost apologetically past the dragon's back at Chrome Hill, and in an attractive but shallow valley south of Crowdecote. But once through the pretty woodlands of Beresford Dale it gets more confident and cuts a deep limestone canyon with cliffs and tors almost equal to those of the more celebrated Dovedale. This canyon is Wolfscote Dale, and it's wilder and more unspoiled than Dovedale, with narrower, less populated paths, and less woodland to hide the crags. Weirs have been constructed to create calm pools that attract trout and grayling to linger.

Compleat Angler

The River Dove here was a particular joy to Charles Cotton, a 17th-century poet born in nearby Beresford Hall. Cotton was also an enthusiastic young angler and introduced his great friend Izaak Walton to the area, teaching him the fine art of fly-fishing. Together they built a fishing temple in the nearby woods of Beresford Dale (in private grounds). They wrote *The Compleat Angler*, a collection of fishing stories published in 1651. Unfortunately Cotton's precarious financial position forced him to sell the hall in 1681, and it now lies in a ruinous state.

The path up Wolfscote Dale begins at Lode Mill, which still has its waterwheel intact. The river, verged by lush vegetation, has cut a deep and twisting valley through the limestone. The slopes are thickly wooded with ash, sycamore and alder. Further north this woodland thins out to reveal more of the crags, and a ravine opens out to the right of Coldeaton Bridge. The dale, like so many in Derbyshire, is rich in wildlife. Dipper, pied wagtails and grey wagtails often forage along the limestone banks, and if you're quick enough you may see the blue flash of a kingfisher diving for a fish. The dale divides again beneath the magnificent Peaseland Rocks. It's a shame to leave the Dove but Biggin Dale is a pleasing contrast. For most of the year it's a dry valley, but in winter the rocky path may be jostling for room with a newly surfaced stream. It's a narrow dale with limestone screes and scrub gorse. What looks like a natural cave on the right is in fact the entrance to an old lead mine. Through a gate you enter a National Nature Reserve, known for its many species of limestone-loving plants and its butterflies. At the top of the dale you come to Biggin, a straggling village, from where the return route is an easy-paced one, using the Tissington Trail, which ambles over the high plains of Alport Moor.

Walk 31

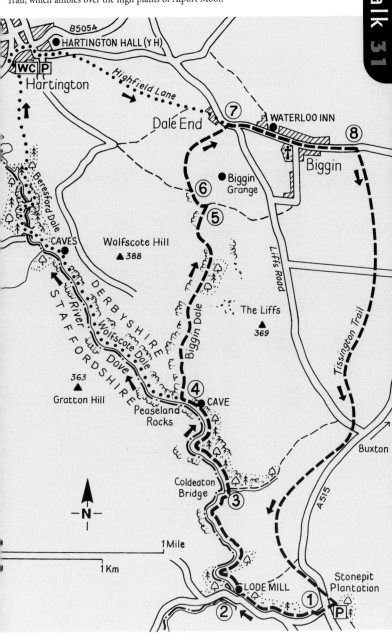

Walk 31

Walk 31 Directions

① From the car park by **Stonepit Plantation**, cross the busy A515 road and follow the **Milldale road** immediately opposite. After a short way you are offered a parallel footpath, keeping you safe from the traffic.

② On reaching the bottom of the dale by **Lode Mill**, turn right along the footpath, tracing the river's east bank through a winding, partially wooded valley.

③ Ignore the footpath on the right at **Coldeaton Bridge**, but instead stay with **Wolfscote Dale** beneath thickly wooded slopes on the right. Beyond a stile the woods cease and the dale becomes bare and rock-fringed, with a cave on the right and the bold pinnacles of **Peaseland Rocks** ahead. Here the valley sides open out into the dry valley of **Biggin Dale**, where this route goes next.

④ The unsignposted path into **Biggin Dale** begins beyond a stile in a cross-wall and climbs by that wall. It continues through scrub woodland and beneath limestone screes. Beyond a gate you enter a nature reserve.

⑤ There's another gate at the far end of the nature reserve. Beyond it the dale curves left, then right,

---

WHERE TO EAT AND DRINK

The **Waterloo Inn** at Biggin is an ideal place for a refreshment break before heading back to Stonepit Plantation. If you're looking for a delicious bar meal at the end of the day, drive a couple of miles south along the A515 to try the **Blue Bell** at Tissington Gate.

---

before dividing again beneath the hill pastures of **Biggin Grange**. We divert left here, over a stile to follow the footpath, signposted to **Hartington**. On the other side of the wall there's a concrete dewpond.

⑥ After 200yds (183m) there's another junction of paths. This time ignore the one signposted to **Hartington** and keep walking straight on, following the path to **Biggin**. It stays with the valley round to the right, passing a small sewage works (on the left) before climbing out of the dale to reach the road at **Dale End**.

⑦ Turn right along the road for a few paces then left, following a road past the **Waterloo Inn** and through **Biggin** village.

WHAT TO LOOK FOR

In Biggin Dale, besides the rampantly prickly gorse bushes you, should see many **limestone loving plants** including the purple-flowered meadow cranesbill, patches of delicate harebells, early purple orchids with their dark-spotted stems and leaves and orangy-yellow cowslips.

---

⑧ Turn right again 500yds (457m) from the village centre on a path that climbs to the **Tissington Trail bridleway**. Follow this old trackbed southwards across the pastures of **Biggin** and **Alport** moors. After 2 miles (3.2km) you reach the car park at **Stonepit Plantation**.

Extending the Walk

The obvious choice is to leave the main route at Point ④ and continue along the River Dove through into **Beresford Dale**, then on into **Hartington**. Leave the village by **Highfield Lane** and you can rejoin the route at Point ⑦ to return to the start of the walk.

Ghosts of Miller's Dale

The rural serenity of modern Miller's Dale belies its early role in the Industrial Revolution.

•DISTANCE•	6 miles (9.7km)
•MINIMUM TIME•	4hrs
•ASCENT / GRADIENT•	690ft (210m) ▲▲▲
•LEVEL OF DIFFICULTY•	
•PATHS•	Generally well-defined paths and tracks, path in Water-cum-Jolly Dale liable to flooding, quite a few stiles
•LANDSCAPE•	Limestone dales
•SUGGESTED MAP•	aqua3 OS Explorer OL24 White Peak
•START / FINISH•	Grid reference: SK 154743
•DOG FRIENDLINESS•	Dogs could run free in dales with no livestock, but kept under control when crossing farmland
•PARKING•	Tideswell Dale pay car park
•PUBLIC TOILETS•	At car park

BACKGROUND TO THE WALK

It's all quiet in Miller's Dale these days, but it wasn't always so. Many early industrialists wanted to build their cotton mills in the countryside, far away from the marauding Luddites of the city. The Wye and its tributaries had the power to work these mills. The railway followed, and that brought more industry with it. And so little Miller's Dale and its neighbours joined the Industrial Revolution.

The walk starts in Tideswell Dale. Nowadays it's choked with thickets and herbs but they hide a history of quarrying and mining. Here the miners wanted basalt, a dark, hard igneous rock that was used for road building.

Cruelty at the Mill

No doubt Litton Mill will eventually be modernised into holiday cottages or executive apartments, but today it lies damp and derelict in a shadowy part of the dale. *The Memoirs of Robert Blincoe*, written in 1863, tells of mill owner Ellis Needham's cruelty to child apprentices, who were often shipped in from the poorhouses of London. Many of the children died and were buried in the churchyards of Tideswell and Taddington. It is said that ghosts of some of the apprentices still make appearances in or around the mill. The walk emerges from the shadows of the mill into Water-cum-Jolly Dale. At first the river is lined by mudbanks thick with rushes and common horsetail. It's popular with wildfowl. The river widens out and, at the same time, impressive limestone cliffs squeeze the path. The river's widening is artificial, a result of it being controlled to form a head of water for the downstream mill.

Round the next corner is Cressbrook Mill, built by Sir Richard Arkwright, but taken over by William Newton. Newton also employed child labour but was said to have treated them well. The rooftop bell tower would have peeled to beckon the apprentices, who lived next door, to the works. Like Litton this impressive Georgian mill was allowed to moulder, but is now being restored as flats. The walk leaves the banks of the Wye at Cressbrook to take

Walk 32

in pretty Cressbrook Dale. In this nature reserve you'll see lily-of-the-valley, wild garlic and bloody cranesbill; you should also see bee and fragrant orchids. Just as you think you've found your true rural retreat you'll climb to the rim of the dale, look across it and see the grassed-over spoil heaps of lead mines. Finally, the ancient strip fields of Litton form a mosaic of pasture and dry-stone wall on the return to Tideswell Dale.

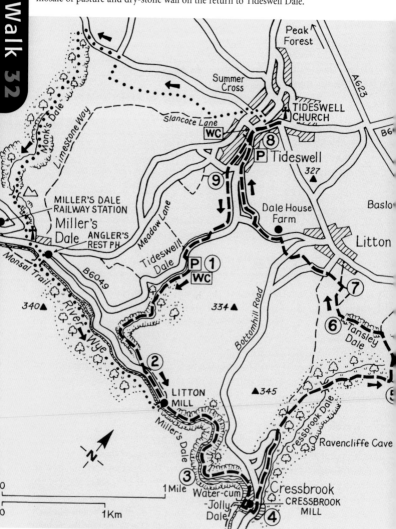

Walk 32 Directions

① Follow the path southwards from beside the car park's toilet block into **Tideswell Dale**, taking the right-hand fork to cross over the little bridge.

② On entering **Miller's Dale**, go left along the tarmac lane to **Litton Mill**. Go through the gateposts on to a concessionary path through the mill yard. Beyond the mill, the path follows the **River Wye**, as it meanders through the tight, steep-sided dale.

Walk 32

③ The river widens out in **Water-cum-Jolly Dale** and the path, liable to flooding here, traces a wall of limestone cliffs before reaching **Cressbrook**. Do not cross the bridge on the right, but turn left to pass in front of **Cressbrook Mill** and out on to the road.

④ Turn left along the road, then take the right fork which climbs steadily into **Cressbrook Dale**. Where the road doubles back uphill leave it for a track going straight ahead into the woods. The track degenerates into a narrow path that emerges in a clearing high above the stream. Follow it downhill to a footbridge over the stream, then take the right fork path, which climbs high up the valley side to a stile in the top wall.

> **WHILE YOU'RE THERE** ⓘ
> **Miller's Dale Railway Station** is a fascinating old site with a good deal of information on the railway, the wildlife and the walking. The station was built in 1863 for the Midland Railway. The line closed in 1967 and wild flowers now line the sides of the trackbed.

⑤ Do not cross the stile, but take the downhill path to the dale bottom, where there's a junction of paths. The one wanted here recrosses the stream on stepping stones, and climbs into **Tansley Dale**.

⑥ The path turns right at the top of the dale, follows a tumbledown wall before crossing it on a step stile. Head for a wall corner in the next field, then veer right through a narrow enclosure to reach a walled track just south of **Litton village**.

⑦ Turn left along the track, which comes out on to a country lane at the crown of a sharp bend. Keep

> **WHAT TO LOOK FOR** ⓘ
> Cressbrook Dale is part of the Derbyshire Dales National Nature Reserve. On the limestone grassland you may see orchids, cranesbill, mountain pansy, globeflower and spring sandwort. One of the many limestone-loving plants is the **Nottingham catchfly**, which loves dry, stony places. The white flowers roll back in daytime, but are fragrant at night. Small insects are often caught on the sticky stalks but nature is being wasteful, for they're never devoured by the plant.

straight on down the lane but leave it at the next bend for a cross-field path to **Bottomfield Road**. Across the road, a further field path descends to the lane at **Dale House Farm**. Turn left, then right on a lane marked unsuitable for motors. Follow this road into **Tideswell**.

⑧ After looking around the village head south down the main street, then right on to **Gordon Road**, which then heads south.

⑨ Where this ends, continue down the stony track ahead, which runs parallel with the main road. Watch for a stile on the left, which gives access to a path, down to the road into **Tideswell Dale**. Turn right along the road, back to the car park.

Extending the Walk
If it's dry you can extend this walk though **Monk's Dale**. Leave the main route at Point ⑧ in **Tideswell** and rejoin it from the **Monsal Trail**, back at **Litton Mill**, near Point ②, to retrace your steps to the start.

> **WHERE TO EAT AND DRINK** ⓘ
> The atmospheric **Anglers Rest** pub at Miller's Dale and the **Hills and Dales Tearooms** in Tideswell are both recommended for their warm welcome to weary walkers.

Walk 33

Hardcastle Crags & Crimsworth Dean

A pair of beautiful wooded valleys, linked by a high level path.

•DISTANCE•	5 miles (8km)
•MINIMUM TIME•	2hrs 30min
•ASCENT / GRADIENT•	787ft (240m) ▲▲▲
•LEVEL OF DIFFICULTY•	
•PATHS•	Good paths and tracks, plus open pasture, no stiles
•LANDSCAPE•	Woodland, fields and moorland fringe
•SUGGESTED MAP•	aqua3 OS Explorer OL21 South Pennines
•START / FINISH•	Grid reference: SD 988291
•DOG FRIENDLINESS•	Plenty of opportunities for dogs to be off lead
•PARKING•	National Trust pay-and-display car parks at Midgehole, near Hebden Bridge (accessible via A6033, Keighley Road)
•PUBLIC TOILETS•	Near car park

BACKGROUND TO THE WALK

Hebden Bridge, just 4 miles (6.4km) from the Yorkshire/Lancashire border, has been a popular place to visit ever since the railway was extended across the Pennines, through the Calder Valley. But those train passengers weren't coming for a day out in a grimy little mill town; the big attraction was the wooded valley of Hebden Dale – usually called 'Hardcastle Crags' – just a short charabanc ride away. 'Hebden Bridge for Hardcastle Crags' was the stationmaster's cry, as trains approached the station. Here were shady woods, easy riverside walks and places to spread out a picnic blanket. To people who lived in the terraced streets of Bradford, Leeds or Halifax, Hardcastle Crags must have seemed idyllic. The steep-sided valley reminded Swiss visitors of their own country, and became 'Little Switzerland' – at least to the writers of tourist brochures. The only disappointment, in fact, was the crags themselves: unassuming gritstone outcrops, almost hidden by trees.

Industrial Demands

The Industrial Revolution created a huge demand for water: for mills, factories and domestic use. To quench the thirst of the rapidly expanding textile towns, many steep-sided valleys, known in the South Pennines as cloughs, were dammed to create reservoirs. Six of these lie within easy walking distance of Hardcastle Crags. They represented huge feats of civil engineering by the hundreds of navvies who built them, around the end of the 19th century, with picks and shovels. The men were housed in a shanty town, known as Dawson City and both men and materials were transported to the work-sites by a convoluted steam-powered railway system that crossed the valley on an elaborate wooden viaduct.

Hardcastle Crags escaped the indignity of being turned into a reservoir, but it was touch and go. Three times during the last 50 years (the last time was in 1970) plans were drawn up to flood the valley. And three times, thankfully, wiser counsels prevailed and the plans were turned down. Lord Savile, a major landowner in the area, once owned the valley. It was he who supplemented the natural woodland with plantings of new trees – particularly pines, and laid out the walks and the carriage drive. In 1948 Lord Savile donated Hardcastle Crags, and the nearby valley of Crimsworth Dean, to the National Trust. Because of this bequeathment, the future of this delightful valley looks secure and local people will continue to enjoy this valuable amenity.

Hardcastle Crags are a haven for wildlife. Bird watchers can look out for pied flycatchers, woodpeckers, jays, sparrowhawks and the ubiquitous dipper – which never strays from the environs of Hebden Water. In spring there are displays of bluebells; in summer the woods are filled with bird-song; the beech woods are a riot of colour as the leaves turn each autumn.

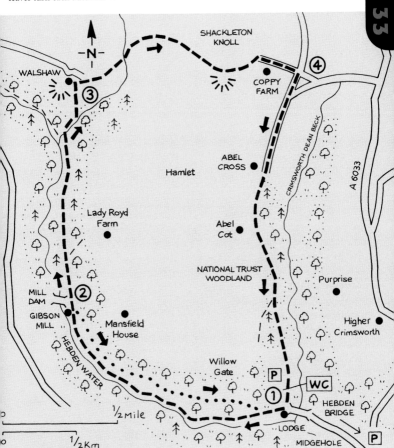

Walk 33 Directions

① Walk up the drive, passing the lodge, and into the woods. Take the first path to the left, which descends to **Hebden Water**. Follow a good riverside path through delectable woodland, passing **Hebden Hey** –

a popular picnic site, with stepping stones – to reach **Gibson Mill**. The buildings, and mill dam behind, are worth investigating.

② For this longer walk you join the track uphill, to the right of **Gibson Mill**, soon passing the crags that give the woods their name.

Walk 33

Keep on the main track, ignoring side-paths, to leave woodland and meet a metalled road. Keep left here, still uphill, across a beck and approach **Walshaw**, a knot of houses enjoying terrific views.

③ Just before you reach the houses – when you are opposite some barns – bear sharp right through a gate on to an enclosed track (signed to **Crimsworth Dean**). You are soon on a grassy track across pasture, descending to a beck and through a gate. Walk uphill, soon bearing to the right as you follow a wall around the shoulder of **Shackleton Hill**. Go through a gate in the wall on your left, and continue as the path bears right, still following the wall, but now it's on your right. Here you have level walking and great views. Take a gate in a wall on the right, just above **Coppy Farm**, to join a walled track downhill into the valley of

Crimsworth Dean. You meet a more substantial track by another ruin of a farm. This track is the old road from Hebden Bridge to Haworth: a great walk to contemplate for another day.

④ Bear right, along this elevated track, passing a farm on the left. Look out, by a farm access track to the right, for **Abel Cross**: not one but a pair of old waymarker stones. Continue down the main track, into National Trust woodland, keeping left, after a field, when the track forks. Beyond a pair of cottages the track is metalled; you soon arrive back at the car parks at **Midgehole**.

Hebden Water & Gibson Mill

One of the finest woodland walks in West Yorkshire.
See map and information panel for Walk 33

•DISTANCE•	2½ miles (4km)
•MINIMUM TIME•	1hr 30min
•ASCENT / GRADIENT•	66ft (20m)
•LEVEL OF DIFFICULTY•	

Walk 34 Directions (Walk 33 option)

If you only have time to walk to Gibson Mill and back, you will have enjoyed arguably the finest short woodland walk in West Yorkshire. The mill was built 200 years ago, when Hebden Water was harnessed to turn a waterwheel and power the cotton spinning machines. The mill pond, behind the mill itself, was built to maintain a good supply of water, even when the river levels were low. This was not the only mill in the valley, but it's the only one still standing. Gibson Mill itself occupies a romantic setting, deep in the woods, its image reflected in the adjacent mill pond. But appearances can be deceptive.

The mill was notorious for its poor working conditions. From a report of 1833 we learn that the 22 employees in Gibson Mill were accustomed to a 72-hour week, with children as young as 10 starting their working day at 6AM and finishing at 7:30PM. Because of their size the children were able to make repairs to the machines while they were still running. Accidents were common. The children had just two breaks during their day – for breakfast and dinner. It wasn't until 1847 that legislation was passed, to limit the working day for women and children to 'only' ten hours. The waterwheel stopped turning in 1852, when the mill was converted to steam power. But by the 1890s the mill had become redundant. Due to its attractive situation, however, it was put to a variety of recreational uses. At various times up to World War Two, it was a tea room, dance hall, dining saloon, even a roller skating rink. The mill pond became a rowing lake. The National Trust now has plans to restore the building into an environmental centre.

Follow the track from the car park at **Midgeley**, up into the woods. Take the first path on the left, after the gatehouse, down to accompany **Hebden Water** upstream. Follow the riverside path passing **Hebden Hey,** a popular picnic site, and two more sets of stepping stones before you arrive at **Gibson Mill**.

Many good paths and tracks converge here, and all provide excellent walking. But for this short ramble you should join the sandy track (known as the carriage drive) that passes the mill. Walk to the right, still through woodland, as the track leads you back to the car park.

A Walk Around Newmillerdam

A pleasant oasis, close to Wakefield, and a chance to feed the ducks.

•DISTANCE•	4½ miles (7.2km)
•MINIMUM TIME•	2hrs
•ASCENT / GRADIENT•	164ft (50m) ▲ ▲ ▲
•LEVEL OF DIFFICULTY•	
•PATHS•	Good paths by lake and through woodland, 2 stiles
•LANDSCAPE•	Reservoir, heath and woodland
•SUGGESTED MAP•	aqua3 OS Explorer 278 Sheffield & Barnsley
•START / FINISH•	Grid reference: SE 331157
•DOG FRIENDLINESS•	Can be off lead on most of walk
•PARKING•	Pay-and-display car park at western end of dam, on A61 between Wakefield and Barnsley
•PUBLIC TOILETS•	At start of walk

Walk 35 Directions

Newmillerdam Country Park lies on the A61 near the village of Newmillerdam, and just 3 miles (4.8km) south of Wakefield. The name refers, unsurprisingly, to a 'new mill on the dam' – a mill where people brought their corn to be ground. The lake and woods were created as a park for a 16th-century country house, which has since been demolished. From 1753 the park formed part of the Chevet Estate, which was owned by the Pilkington family. They used the lake for fishing and shooting and,

in 1820, built a distinctive boathouse as a place for their guests to socialise and enjoy the lake view. This Grade II listed building has recently been restored and is now used as a visitor centre.

In 1954 Newmillerdam became a public park; local people come here to walk, fish, watch birds or just feed the ducks. The lake is surrounded by woodland. Conifer trees were planted here during the 1950s with the intention, once the trees had reached maturity, to use the wood for making pit props for the coal mines. These trees are mature now but, ironically, the need for the pit props has gone, as most of the Yorkshire pits are closed. The Wakefield Countryside Service is gradually replacing the conifers with broadleaved trees such as oak, ash, birch and hazel, which support a greater variety of birdlife.

A simple circuit of the lake is a pleasant 2-mile (3.2km) stroll, on

---

WHERE TO EAT AND DRINK ℹ

You can sit outside the **Dam Inn** where they offer good food, including a carvery, conveniently and appropriately, by the lake's dam. The **Fox and Hounds** and the **Pledwick Well** make up the trio of pubs in reasonably close proximity to Newmillerdam though neither are especially dog friendly.

Walk 35

WHAT TO LOOK FOR

Ducks, geese and swans have no trouble finding food at Newmillerdam, as people with bagfuls of stale bread queue up to feed them. The most common of the ducks you'll see is the **mallard**, the 'basic' duck. The females are brown and make the satisfying *quack quack* sounds which delight children. The males have distinctive green heads, yellow bills and grey bodies. Their tone is more nasal and much weaker sounding. Mallards pair off in the late autumn but the males leave egg incubation and rearing of the young to the females.

a track that is suitable for push-chairs or wheelchairs. But this walk also takes you through **Seckar Wood**, a Site of Special Scientific Interest (SSSI). The woodland comprises a mixture of dry heath, wet heath and scrubland: another habitat rich in wildlife. During the late summer months the heathland displays a colourful profusion of purple heather.

Walk right, along the A61, to the far side of the lake, to join a path down the eastern side of the lake. Pass the ornate boathouse and a causeway across the lake. Where the lake narrows to a beck, take a bridge across it. Ignore paths to left and right, by walking straight ahead, up into mixed woodland. Bear left when you come to a more substantial track, turning right after 250yds (228m) to take a bridge over the trackbed of an old railway line. Continue on a track ahead, soon

following a chain-link fence on your right, to arrive at the A61 road again. Cross the road and walk right for 250yds (228m) before taking a path left past a metal gate and into **Seckar Wood**. Pass a couple of ponds and make a gradual ascent up through the wood; at the top the trees give way to heather and heathland. Ignore all side-tracks and leave the heath as you meet another path.

Go right here, with a hedge on the left and a wall on the right. Soon you find yourself on a field path. Follow the edge of the wood downhill, as it sweeps right, down to a stile at the bottom of the field. Cross this stile and another immediately after; at the next field keep right until you come to a gap in the hedge. Now follow a grassy path at the field's edge, keeping the hedgerow to your left.

As you approach houses, follow the track and the hedge to the right. At a wide gap in the hedge, go left on a farm track that brings you out on to a road. Go right here, downhill, turning right after 200yds (192m) at a mini-roundabout, on to **Wood Lane**. Just past the **Pennine Camphill Community** take a footpath on the left between a fence and a wall. Meet a minor road by a sharp bend. Walk straight ahead, down the road, to reach the A61. Go left, back down to the car park at **Newmillerdam**.

WHILE YOU'RE THERE

Immediately to the north of Newmillerdam is **Pugneys Country Park**, a popular place of recreation with people from Wakefield. A large lake is overlooked by what remains of Sandal Castle, which was, in the words of the old music hall song, 'one of the ruins that Cromwell knocked about a bit'. The original motte and bailey date from the 12th century, the later stone castle from the days of Richard III. He had planned to make Sandal his key permanent stronghold in the north of England before he was killed at the Battle of Bosworth in 1485.

Walk 36

Through Scarborough's Raincliffe Woods

Just outside Scarborough, a walk through woodland to the rare remains of a glacial lake.

•DISTANCE•	5 miles (8km)
•MINIMUM TIME•	2hrs
•ASCENT / GRADIENT•	584ft (175m) ▲▲▲
•LEVEL OF DIFFICULTY•	
•PATHS•	Field tracks, woodland paths, some steep, 2 stiles
•LANDSCAPE•	Farmland and hillside woodland
•SUGGESTED MAP•	aqua3 OS Explorer OL27 North York Moors – Eastern
•START / FINISH•	Grid reference: SE 984875
•DOG FRIENDLINESS•	Can be off lead in most of woodland
•PARKING•	Hazelhead picnic site on Mowthorpe Road, near road junction
•PUBLIC TOILETS•	None on route

BACKGROUND TO THE WALK

The steep hillside of Raincliffe Woods overlooks a deep valley carved out in the ice ages. Although mostly replanted in the 1950s and 60s, the woods in places retain remnants of ancient oak and heather woodland – look out for the heather and bilberry bushes beneath oak trees that will show you where.

The Paths of the Aristocracy

The woods have long been open to the public, though in the 19th century they were privately owned by the 1st Earl of Londesborough, and some of the roads and tracks were named after his family – Lady Edith's Drive after his wife and Lady Mildred's Ride after her sister. Lord Londesborough was the grandfather of Edith, Osbert and Sacheverell Sitwell. Osbert recalled in his autobiography *Left Hand Right Hand!* how he and Edith were taken in the early years of the 20th century on hair-raising drives by their grandfather in his buckboard through Raincliffe Woods. They would then walk up the steep hillsides through columbine and honeysuckle. Unfortunately, they often became lost, and the Earl's language was, for a time, immoderate, until he remembered the children's presence.

Throxenby Mere

Beetle enthusiasts wax lyrical about Throxenby Mere. The last vestiges of the huge glacial lake that formed more than 15,000 years ago, after the ice age, it contains species of rare water-beetles, and is one of the places in the North of England to which coleopterists (beetle students to the layman) make tracks. You will also find the distinctive pinky-purple flowers and wide leaves of the broad-leaved willow-herb on its fringes.

Throughout the walk you will come upon humps and banks, depressions and pits that show that this hillside has been a hive of human activity in the past. As the path approaches Throxenby Mere it crosses part of a Bronze-Age dyke system, while elsewhere are medieval banks and the remains of pits for charcoal burning. You will also pass a small quarry which was used for local building stone.

The Sea Cut

In the valley below Raincliffe Woods is the Sea Cut, or North Back Drain, a flood relief channel that runs 3 miles (4.8km) from the River Derwent to Scalby Beck. Engineered in 1806 by local man Sir George Caley, it takes excess water from the Derwent to the sea at Scalby to prevent flooding in the Vale of Pickering. Operation is by means of a sluice gate (now remotely-controlled) 825yds (750m) west of Mowthorpe Bridge near the beginning of the walk. When in operation, it restores the Derwent's link to the sea that was lost when glacial deposits blocked its original route.

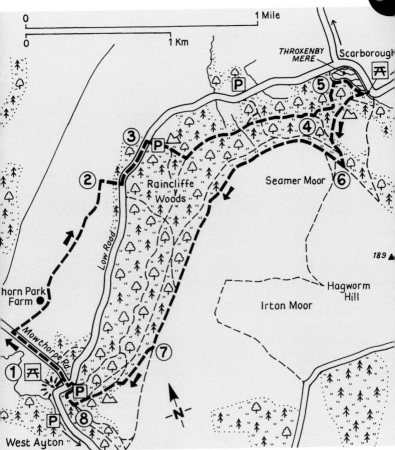

Walk 36 Directions

① From the picnic site, walk on to the road and turn left, downhill. After the woodland ends, pass houses on the right, then opposite a

bungalow, No 5, turn right down a track to **Thorn Park Farm**. Follow the track as it bends left by the farm buildings, then right past a cottage to a metal gate. Continue to follow the track, which bends left then right, then through two gateways.

Walk 36

② Just before the next gateway turn right and walk up the field side to a stile beside a gateway, which takes you on a short path to the road. Turn left. Follow the road to the next **car park** on the right.

③ Go up through the car park towards the gate and uphill on the path ahead. Where the main path bends right, go straight ahead, more steeply, to reach a crossing, grassy track. Turn left through a gate and follow the path. Where it forks, take the right-hand path.

④ Look out for a path on the left, which immediately bends right over a **drainage runnel**. The path goes down into a small valley. Turn left, downhill, then follow the path as it bends right again, past an old quarry. The path descends to reach

Throxenby Mere. Turn right along the edge of the Mere – part of the path is on boardwalks.

⑤ Just before you reach a picnic place, turn right through an area bare of undergrowth to take a path which goes up steeply until it reaches a grassy track at the top of the hill.

⑥ Turn right and go through a metal gate, then follow the path for a mile (1.6km), parallel with the wall. It passes through a gateway with a stile by it and eventually reaches a gate with a public bridleway sign.

⑦ Do not go through this gate out into fields, but turn right and continue in the woodland. Where the main path swings left and another goes right, go straight ahead, steeply downhill. When the path joins another go left, down steps and along a boardwalk to meet a crossing path.

⑧ Turn right and go down to a gate into a car park. Turn left on to the road, and left again to reach a road junction. Turn right, following the **Harwood Dale** sign, for **Hazelhead** picnic site.

Gisburn Forest – a Walk in the Woods

Wooded valleys and heathland – accompanied by the sounds of woodland birds and waterfowl.

•DISTANCE•	3 miles (4.8km)
•MINIMUM TIME•	1hr 30min
•ASCENT / GRADIENT•	285ft (87m)
•LEVEL OF DIFFICULTY•	
•PATHS•	Forest tracks and footpaths
•LANDSCAPE•	Wooded valleys, forest, beckside heathland
•SUGGESTED MAP•	aqua3 OS Explorer OL41 Forest of Bowland & Ribblesdale
•START / FINISH•	Grid reference: SD 732565
•DOG FRIENDLINESS•	Fine for dogs under reasonable control
•PARKING•	Stocks Reservoir car park, Gisburn Forest (free of charge)
•PUBLIC TOILETS•	None on route

BACKGROUND TO THE WALK

Perfectly placed between the Yorkshire Dales and the Forest of Bowland, Gisburn Forest in the Upper Hodder Valley is the setting for this short, circular stroll. Don't be put off because it's in a forest – it certainly isn't a dire trek through the darkness of a dense conifer plantation. You will walk along open, naturally wooded valleys, beside a tumbling beck and over heathland. You will have views over the reservoir and up to the fells, and you will hear the woodland birdsong and the call of the wildfowl on the water. If you're lucky, you may spot a deer, footprints in the sandy earth confirm their presence.

Stocks Reservoir

The two defining aspects of this walk are the open waters of Stocks Reservoir and the woodlands of Gisburn Forest. The reservoir was built in the 1930s to provide drinking water for the towns of central Lancashire. The village of Stocks was submerged in the process along with many ancient farmsteads. The date stone from one of these can now be seen over the doorway of the post office in Tosside. It was formed by damming the River Hodder and can hold 2.6 billion gallons (12 billion litres) of water when it is at full capacity.

Ospreys and Peregrines

Attractively placed on the edge of the forest, the reservoir is now an important site for wildfowl and 30 different species visit during the average winter period. Amongst the less-commonly sighted of these are red-throated divers, whooper swans, gadwalls and great crested grebes. Amongst the different birds of prey who frequent the area, ospreys and peregrine falcons have been spotted, as well as a rare passing marsh harrier. A birdwatching hide is provided for budding ornithologists and there's a permissive shoreline footpath.

The Forestry Commission's extensive woodland known as Gisburn Forest was developed at the same time as the reservoir and was opened by HRH Prince George in July 1932. It covers 3,000 acres (1,214ha), making it the largest single forested area in Lancashire.

There are several waymarked trails to be enjoyed and a cycle network has been developed extending to over 10 miles (16km). Although the majority of the plantations are of the monotonous coniferous variety and are managed principally as a commercial crop, more and more broadleaf trees are being planted to improve the visual aspect and to increase the diversity of wildlife. The forest and the reservoir are now managed in tandem, with inputs from United Utilities, the Forestry Commission and local parishes, to develop a sustainable economic base for this beautiful landscape.

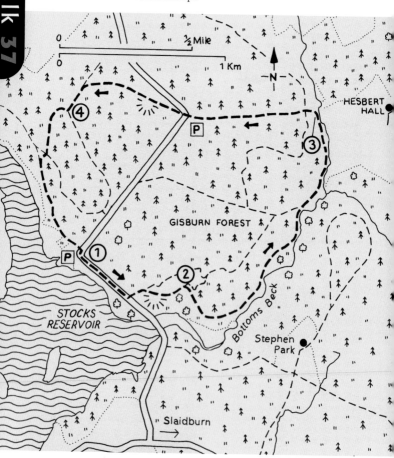

Walk 37 Directions

① Leave **Stocks Reservoir car park** in a south easterly direction (straight ahead from the right of the two vehicular entrances). Walk for approximately ¼ mile (400m) then turn left on a forest track marked with a wooden public footpath sign; a red marker post

soon confirms your route. There are good views right, through the trees to the reservoir and causeway with the fells in the background. Keep on the track as it takes you beside open wooded valleys and through natural woodland with a river down on your right.

② Follow the red marker post, set a little off to the right, as it leads you

Walk 37

WHERE TO EAT AND DRINK ⓘ
Nothing is available within the forest itself, so it might be an idea to pack a picnic. Slaidburn, 4½ miles (7.2km) south, has some cafés and the famous 13th-century **Hark to Bounty Inn** which serves good bar meals but doesn't welcome dogs. **Dunsop Bridge** has cafés and a river flowing by the village green spilling out mallards on to the grass – especially if you are lunching.

down on to a footpath. The footpath continues with a stream on your left, across a low footbridge to the opposite bank. Soon the tumbling peaty **Bottoms Beck** is on your right with patches of reeds to the left, until a raised embankment leads to higher ground as you pass the farmland of **Hesbert Hall** to the right.

③ Follow the next red marker post as it directs you left to leave the beck, and walk just a few paces to cross straight over a forest track. Follow the path as it takes you gently uphill over boardwalks and

heathland, through upright gateposts by an old broken down wall. Walk straight through **Swinshaw Top** car park to the road and go straight over to take a narrow footpath through the woods by another red marker post. The path opens on to a broadish green swathe but is soon closed in again; however lovely elevated views over the reservoir, left, and the fells ahead make the start of your descent pleasurable.

WHILE YOU'RE THERE ⓘ
The **Forest of Bowland** is a designated Area of Outstanding Natural Beauty (AONB) occupying the north eastern corner of Lancashire. It is a landscape of barren gritstone fells, moorland and steep sided valleys, with 3,260 acres (1,320ha) of open country available to walkers. The village of Dunsop Bridge in the Trough of Bowland claims to be the official centre of the country – a telephone box adjacent to the village green marks the precise spot.

④ Meet a forest track at a bend, proceed straight ahead (slightly right) and follow the track for 200yds (183m) until red posts turn you right, down a footpath with a stream on the right. At a T-junction of footpaths, turn left across open heathland on a clear path back to the car park.

WHAT TO LOOK FOR ⓘ
It's more a case of what to listen for! The **birdsong** throughout the walk, from tiny wrens darting into the bushes in front, to the cry of the curlew skyward is symphonic. Add to that the call of the wildfowl on the reservoir, never far away, and the orchestration is complete.

Walk 38

Lilies and Lakes Seen from Loughrigg

Above little Ambleside, Loughrigg Fell looks out to lake, dale and high fell.

•DISTANCE•	3¼ miles (5.3km)
•MINIMUM TIME•	1hr 45min
•ASCENT / GRADIENT•	575ft (175m) ▲▲▲
•LEVEL OF DIFFICULTY•	
•PATHS•	Road, paths and tracks, can be muddy in places, 3 stiles
•LANDSCAPE•	Town, park and open hillside with views to high fells
•SUGGESTED MAP•	aqua3 OS Explorer OL7 The English Lakes (SE)
•START / FINISH•	Grid reference: NY 375047
•DOG FRIENDLINESS•	Under control; busy roads, park, sheep grazing
•PARKING•	Ambleside central car park
•PUBLIC TOILETS•	At car park

BACKGROUND TO THE WALK

The favourite of many, Loughrigg is a delightful low fell, which runs from Ambleside and the head of Windermere lake, towards both Langdale and Grasmere. This circuit crosses the River Rothay by Miller Bridge and rises to a craggy viewpoint before traversing small Lily Tarn to return via the stone lane of Miller Brow.

With the exception of possibly thick mist or cloud, this is a walk for all seasons and most weather conditions. The views, south over Waterhead and down Windermere and north over the wooded vale of Rydal into the high mountain drama of the Fairfield Horseshoe, are some of the most evocative in the region. The delightful detail of tree, rocky knoll, heather, bracken and the white and green cup and saucers of the lilies on Lily Tarn, contrast with the grand open views of mountain, dale and lake.

Ambleside

Even before you reach the heights of lovely Loughrigg, the varied slate stone buildings of Ambleside provide an intriguing start to the walk. Indeed, despite some recent developments, there is still a lot more to this little town than just being the outdoor equipment capital of Britain. Sited in the old county of Westmorland, Ambleside has long been a site of occupation. Bronze-Age remains, from as far back as 2000 BC, can be seen on the nearby fells and the Galava Roman fort, near Waterhead, was one of the most important in north west England.

How Head, just up the Kirkstone road, one of the oldest surviving buildings in old Ambleside, is located in the area known as Above Stock. Sections of this fine stone house date back to the 16th century and it was once the lodge of the Master Forester of the Barony of Kendal. It has massive circular chimneys, a typical Westmorland feature, stone mullioned windows and incorporates stone from the old Roman fort at Waterhead and cobbles from the bed of Stock Ghyll Beck.

Stock Ghyll once served as the heartbeat of the town when, some 150 years ago, it provided water power for 12 watermills. On this walk we pass a restored waterwheel, immediately followed by the famous Bridge House, one of the most photographed buildings in the Lake District. Spanning the beck, this tiny 17th-century building is said to have been built thus to avoid paying land tax. Locally it is said to have once housed a family with six children. It is now a shop and information centre for the National Trust. Ambleside has become a major tourist resort with shops, hotels and restaurants, and is a convenient base for exploring the rest of the Lake District.

Walk 38 **Directions**

① Take the wooden footbridge from the car park and go right, along the Rydal road to pass the

waterwheel and **Bridge House**. At the junction bear right along **Compston Road**. Continue to the next junction, with the cinema on the corner, then bear right to cross the side road and enter **Vicarage**

Walk 38

Road alongside the chip shop. Pass the school and enter **Rothay Park**. Follow the main path through the park to emerge by a flat bridge over **Stock Ghyll Beck**. Cross this then go left to cross over the stone arched **Miller Bridge** spanning the River Rothay.

> **WHILE YOU'RE THERE** ℹ
> The **Armitt Museum**, opposite the car park, provides a fascinating look at Ambleside and its environs in times past. An area is devoted to Beatrix Potter, where her desk and some of her natural history watercolours are on display. **Borrans Park** at Waterhead, with **Galava Roman Fort** next to it, and **Rothay Park** both provide pleasant recreational areas for those with a little time to spare. Near the Bridge House, the **Glass House** provides demonstrations in glass blowing.

② Bear right along the road over the cattle grid until, in a few paces, a steep surfaced road rises to the left. Climb the road, which becomes unsurfaced, by the buildings of **Brow Head**. At the S-bend beyond the buildings, a stone stile leads up and off left. Pass through the trees to find, in a few dozen paces, a stone squeeze stile. Pass through this and climb the open hillside above. The paths are well worn and a variety of routes are possible. For the best views over Windermere keep diagonally left. Rising steeply at first, the path levels before rising again to ascend the first rocky knoll. A higher, larger knoll follows and offers definitive views of the Fairfield Horseshoe to the north and over Windermere to the south.

③ Beyond this, the way descends to the right, dropping to a well-defined path. Follow the path to pass a little pond before cresting a rise and falling to lovely little

> **WHAT TO LOOK FOR** ℹ
> Lily Tarn, just after Point ③, is naturally known for its white **water-lilies**. The lilies have lightly scented white flowers that unfurl between June and September. Despite its great beauty it has a sinister reputation. Whilst its blooms may tempt the inquisitive, rope-like stems which grow up to 8ft (2.4m) long, can easily ensnare the unwary and many a hapless swimmer has been drowned, beguiled by its innocent appearance.

pocket-handkerchief **Lily Tarn** (flowers bloom late June to September). The path skirts the right edge of the tarn, roughly following the crest of **Loughrigg Fell**. A gate/stile leads to the base of a further knoll and this is ascended to another worthy viewpoint.

④ Take the path descending right to a track below. Bear right to a gate which leads through the stone wall boundary of the open fell and into a field. Continue to descend the track, passing an interesting building on the left, the old golf clubhouse. Intercept the original route just above the buildings of **Brow Head**.

> **WHERE TO EAT AND DRINK** ℹ
> Inns, cafés and restaurants and all types of eateries abound in Ambleside. A particular favourite with walkers and climbers is the atmospheric **Golden Rule**, a dog-friendly traditional public house, just up the Kirkstone road above the car park.

⑤ Continue to cross **Miller Bridge** then, before the flat bridge, bear left to follow the track by the side of **Stock Ghyll Beck**. Beyond the meadows a lane through the houses leads to the main Rydal road. Bear right along the road to the car park beyond the fire station.

To Loughrigg Fell Top

A circumnavigation of the shoulder of Loughrigg provides wonderful views.
See map and information panel for Walk 38

•DISTANCE•	5 miles (8km)
•MINIMUM TIME•	2hrs 30min
•ASCENT / GRADIENT•	690ft (210m) ▲▲▲
•LEVEL OF DIFFICULTY•	

Walk 39 Directions (Walk 38 option)

At Point Ⓐ bear left and descend into a rather boggy hollow. Cross the stream and bear right to find the main, largest and most distinct path. Other paths climb more directly above this point and tend to be a little more strenuous. The main path bears right, over **Black Mire**, before curving left to ascend the hillside. Climb steeply to gain a col. Steep craggy outcrops lie to the right. Beyond the col, the path levels and the going eases. Swing slightly left, to round a little tarnlet, then head for a shallow natural corridor, which ascends the high shoulder. Bear left at the head of the slope to find the summit of **Loughrigg Fell** in a few hundred paces. A large cairn and stone trig point stand above the bracken, heather, tarnlets and outcrops.

Even the most discerning hill walker cannot fail to be impressed by the view from Loughrigg Fell. It is staggeringly good, both in terms of distance and in content. From here the high fells of the region, Coniston Old Man, Wetherlam, the Scafells, Bowfell, the Langdale Pikes, Dollywagon Pike, Fairfield and Red Screes, contrast dramatically with the woods, lakes and dales spread below. Those wishing to see the full extent of Grasmere lake may wish to continue walking a little further along the felltop here before returning to the summit.

From the summit return to the top of the shallow corridor taken in the ascent then follow the path that swings away to the left (roughly north east). Pass a little tarnlet before descending by the stream, following another little natural corridor. Bear right and cross the stream just before the going steepens. An easy descent follows and leads to a flat and rather boggy area known as **Scartufts**. Swing left before a little tarnlet and circumnavigate a rocky bracken-covered knoll. Beyond the knoll go right at the junction of paths to take the path heading south. Follow the little footpath over the flat boggy ground to pass another knoll. The path bears slightly left and traverses the left edge of **Black Mire**. The driest alternative from here is to keep left to join a large, distinct stony footpath at the corner of a dry-stone wall. Continue in the same direction following the line of the wall to intercept a track and a gate in the wall. Join the original route of Walk 38 at Point Ⓑ.

Walk 40

Above Kielder's Dam

In the great forest by the vast reservoir, you can capture the essence of two of Britain's biggest human-made creations.

•DISTANCE•	3¼ miles (5.3km)
•MINIMUM TIME•	1hr 45min
•ASCENT / GRADIENT•	197ft (60m)
•LEVEL OF DIFFICULTY•	
•PATHS•	Mostly rubble-surfaced tracks
•LANDSCAPE•	Lake surrounded by forested hills
•SUGGESTED MAP•	aqua3 OS Explorer OL42 Kielder Water & Forest
•START / FINISH•	Grid reference: NY 706883
•DOG FRIENDLINESS•	Dogs can be off lead
•PARKING•	Large car park at Hawkhope
•PUBLIC TOILETS•	At car park

Walk 40 Directions

The most westerly limits of Northumberland are defined by the tortuous meanderings of the Scottish border. Here, where the population, already thin, reaches its lowest density, is the largest non-natural forest in Britain. And within this forest is northern Europe's largest non-natural lake.

The Percy and Swinburne families owned much of the land around the valley of the River North Tyne and the Percys built Kielder Castle as a shooting lodge in 1775. During the 19th century, coal was mined on land now submerged by the reservoir. Some was used locally, while a good proportion was carried, by packhorse and later by railway, for sale across the border.

By the mid-1930s, mining had come to an end, but was set to be replaced by a new industry. In 1919, the Forestry Commission was formed to cater for Britain's timber

needs. In 1924 it bought 2,000 acres (810ha) near Falstone and, in 1932, a further 47,000 acres (19,035ha). Following World War Two, more land was acquired and planting extended. To house the workers needed for this rapidly expanding enterprise, forestry villages were built at Kielder, in the centre of the forest, and at Byrness and Stonehaugh near its eastern edges.

The various plantations that are now linked together to make up Kielder Forest cover a total area of 100,000 acres (40,500ha). The trees are made up almost entirely of five conifer species: Norway and sitka spruce, Scots and lodgepole pine

WHAT TO LOOK FOR ⓘ
The best viewpoint on this walk is from the top of the **Belling Crag**, which juts out over the lake shore. The crag is made of fell sandstone and was once an important rock climbing venue, with about two dozen routes on its steep faces. However, because of the construction of the reservoir, climbing is no longer possible here.

and Japanese larch. Kielder Castle is now the administrative headquarters of Forest Enterprise, and also houses a visitors' information centre.

In 1974, the order was made authorising the construction of Kielder Reservoir, to provide water for the cities and industries of the north east. Work began in 1975 and was completed five years later. In December 1980, Kielder Water began to fill up, and the scheme was officially opened in May 1982.

> **WHERE TO EAT AND DRINK** ℹ️
> Pets are welcome at the nearby **Blackcock Inn** at Falstone. This 18th-century pub serves a range of bar meals as well as more formal dining and boasts an enviable array of ales.

The dam is ¾ mile (1.2km) long and 170ft (52m) high. The shoreline encloses a lake 7 miles (11.3km) in length and has a capacity of 44 billion gallons (200 billion litres). Water is released through the valve tower, which rises from the lake 190yds (174m) from the dam. It flows into the North Tyne and from there to the Tyne. Some of the water is extracted at Riding Mill and pumped through a tunnel under the Durham moors into the Wear and the Tees.

Controversy generated by the building of the reservoir has been silenced by the lake's recreational value and its undoubted enhancement of the scenery of the North Tyne Valley.

From the western end of Hawkhope car park, take the north shore footpath through the trees and on to the rubble-covered forest road. Follow this to the left. After 100yds

(91m), go down the track on the left to the lake shore. This track zig-zags, generally parallel to the shoreline, over a small footbridge and past the remains of a **bastle** (fortified farm building). Follow the wooden waymarkers round an inlet of the lake and over two footbridges to the furthest reach of the inlet.

Follow the track on the left, which leads across a narrow isthmus on to the Belling peninsula. At a fork in the track, go right and continue around the shore of **The Belling**. There are excellent views across the lake from several points and at one viewpoint there is a reconstruction of a corbelled beehive hut.

After re-crossing the isthmus, you come to a fork in the track. Follow the left fork uphill to a junction with a larger track and turn left at a ruined sheep pen. This track leads, in 110yds (100m) back on to the main forest road. Follow this to the left, gently uphill. From the upper levels of the road, where the forest has been cleared, there are views of the lake and one of its larger inlets.

> **WHILE YOU'RE THERE** ℹ️
> Near the southern end of the dam, a track of ½ mile (800m) leads uphill to **Falstone Moss**. This is a small nature reserve and Site of Special Scientific Interest (SSSI), and is the most accessible of a number of sites in Kielder Forest, known as the Border Mires.

At the highest point, turn right on to a partly overgrown track. Follow this for 1½ miles (2.4km) until you come to a rubble track at **High Hawkhope**. Turn right and, after a few hundred paces, right again. Continue to the dam, which is now clearly visible in front of you. The car park lies just beyond the dam.

Remembering the Reivers at Newcastleton

A quiet walk through borderlands where cattle raiding was once a part of everyday life for the local inhabitants.

•DISTANCE•	5 miles (8km)
•MINIMUM TIME•	2hrs
•ASCENT / GRADIENT•	689ft (210m) ▲▲▲
•LEVEL OF DIFFICULTY•	
•PATHS•	Quiet byroads and farm tracks, one rough climb
•LANDSCAPE•	Rolling borderlands and moors
•SUGGESTED MAP•	aqua3 OS Explorer 324 Liddesdale & Kershope Forest
•START / FINISH•	Grid reference: NY 483875
•DOG FRIENDLINESS•	Can mostly run free, Carby Hill not good for older dogs
•PARKING•	Douglas Square
•PUBLIC TOILETS•	Langholm Street, next to fire station

BACKGROUND TO THE WALK

It might seem quiet today, but the area around Newcastleton was once what tabloid newspapers would now describe as 'war-torn'. Ownership of these borderlands was hotly disputed between England and Scotland for hundreds of years and there were frequent battles and skirmishes. You'll pass a reminder of those turbulent days on this walk.

Raids and Revenge

Because places like Newcastleton were so remote from the centres of power in both London and Edinburgh, they were not only difficult to defend, they also had a reputation for lawlessness. Feuds often developed between powerful local families and violent raids, and cases of cattle rustling (reiving), were common – cattle were then a valuable asset. These were ruthless people who could probably have shown the Vikings a thing or two about raping and pillaging.

A raid would commonly be followed by an illegal revenge attack (which of course was better fun, being illegal) or sometimes a legal 'Hot Trod'. This was a pursuit mounted immediately after a raid and had strict rules – including one stating that a lighted turf had to be carried if the trod crossed the border. When reivers were caught they were often taken hostage (the ransom money was very handy), taken prisoner, or even killed. Not surprisingly the countryside became studded with sturdy castles and fortified 'pele' towers, so that people could better defend themselves.

The most powerful family in this area were the Armstrongs, the principal reiving clan in the Borders. They were extremely influential and held large tracts of land. Their main seat was Mangerton Tower, the rather pitiful remains of which you can see on this walk. The Armstrongs were said to be able to muster 3,000 mounted men whenever they wished to launch a raid into England. They were ruthless and violent, running a rather successful protection racket as one of their money-making ventures. Imagine the mafia with cows and you'll get the picture.

Controlling the Clans

It wasn't until the Union of the Crowns took place in 1603, following the death of Queen Elizabeth I, that the Border wars ceased and the power of the reiving clans was finally dispersed. Keen to gain control and make his mark as an effective ruler of the new united kingdom, James VI of Scotland (James I of England) banned weapons and established mounted forces to police the area. Reiving families – often identified with the help of local informers – were scattered and members transported or even executed.

After Archibald Armstrong of Mangerton was executed in 1610, the Armstrongs lost their lands to the Scotts, another powerful local family. However, the family didn't disappear and members of this once fearsome tribe have continued to make their mark on the world. Most famous of all must be Neil Armstrong, who carried a fragment of Armstrong tartan when he stepped on to the surface of the moon, in 1969.

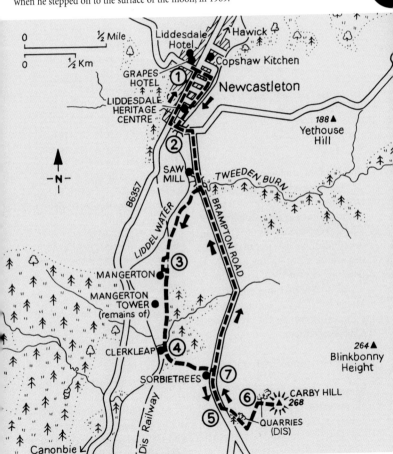

Walk 41 Directions

① From **Douglas Square**, with your back to the **Grapes Hotel**, walk along **Wyitchester Street** (or any other street opposite) and go down to the **Liddel Water**. Turn right, walk along the riverbank and join the path downstream to reach the bridge. Turn left at the top of the steps and cross the bridge.

② After about 100yds (91m), turn right and follow the **Brampton Road**, passing static caravans on either side. You'll eventually pass an old sawmill with a corrugated iron roof and will then reach the **Tweeden Burn bridge**. Cross the bridge and walk uphill, then turn right and join the metalled track that leads to **Mangerton farm**. Continue on this road until you

---

WHERE TO EAT AND DRINK ⓘ

You've got a few choices in Newcastleton. There's the **Grapes Hotel** on Douglas Square or the **Liddesdale Hotel**, also on Douglas Square, both of which serve bar meals. You can also try the **Copshaw Kitchen**, a coffee shop and licensed restaurant, which is on North Hermitage Street.

---

near the farm buildings.

③ You now turn left, then sharp right, and walk down on to the bed of the old railway line, which has joined you from the right. This line once linked Carlisle to Edinburgh but was closed following the Beeching cuts of 1963. Follow the line as it leads past the remains of **Mangerton Tower**, in a field to your right, and continue until you reach **Clerkleap cottage**.

④ Turn left immediately after the

WHAT TO LOOK FOR ⓘ

You'll probably notice plenty of **stinging nettles** as you walk along the old railway line. That's because they love to grow on disturbed ground and flourish in environments such as this. They're a real favourite of **butterflies** such as the red admiral as they provide a juicy source of food for their caterpillars.

---

cottage, then go through the wooden gate to join a rough track. This leads through woodland and on, uphill, to join the road by **Sorbietrees farm**. Turn right now and walk along the road, past the farm, to a small stand of conifers on the left. Turn left through the gate.

⑤ Bear right now and head up the left-hand side of the trees. Walk past the top of the wood and a former quarry, to reach a dry-stone wall. Turn left and follow the wall uphill, crossing it about 437yds (400m) ahead at a convenient right-angle bend.

⑥ It's a bit of a scramble now, over bracken and scree, to reach the summit – the views are great though. Known locally as **Caerba Hill**, this was once the site of a prehistoric settlement. You now have to retrace your steps to reach the road again, then turn right and

---

WHILE YOU'RE THERE ⓘ

Liddesdale Heritage Centre and Museum is the place to come to learn more about the history of the area and its people. Trainspotters will love the Waverley Line memorabilia, which includes a seat from the station platform and an old railway clock. And if you're trying to trace your family tree you can make use of their genealogical records.

---

walk back to **Sorbietrees farm**.

⑦ At the farm, continue on the main road as it bears right and follow it back over the **Tweeden bridge** and up to the **Holm Bridge**. Cross the bridge and walk straight on for 100yds (91m), then turn right on to the **B6357** and walk back to the village square via the little **heritage centre**.

The Solway Shore from Carsethorn to Arbigland

Visit the birthplace of John Paul Jones, the 'father of the American Navy'.

Walk 42

•DISTANCE•	5½ miles (8.8km)
•MINIMUM TIME•	2hrs 30min
•ASCENT / GRADIENT•	82ft (25m)
•LEVEL OF DIFFICULTY•	
•PATHS•	Rocky seashore, woodland tracks and country roads
•LANDSCAPE•	Seashore, woodland and pasture
•SUGGESTED MAP•	aqua3 OS Explorer 313 Dumfries & Dalbeattie, New Abbey
•START / FINISH•	Grid reference: NX 993598
•DOG FRIENDLINESS•	Good walk for dogs
•PARKING•	Car park by beach at Carsethorn
•PUBLIC TOILETS•	At John Paul Jones Museum

BACKGROUND TO THE WALK

The man hailed in the USA as the 'father of the American Navy' was born John Paul in a poor gardener's cottage at Arbigland, on the Solway coast in 1745.

Young Seaman

At the age of 13 John signed up as an apprentice seaman journeying to Virginia on the *Friendship of Whitehaven*. He later signed on as third mate on a slave ship, the *King George of Whitehaven*. He lasted two years and advanced to first mate before he quit in disgust with the slave trade. On his passage home he acquired his first command when the captain and mate of his vessel died of fever. As the only qualified man left, John took control and brought the ship safely home. The owners rewarded him with permanent command. He had a reputation for a fiery temper and was once charged with murder but found not guilty. In 1773 he fled the West Indies, after killing the ringleader of a mutiny, and went to Virginia where he had inherited some property. It was around this time that he changed his name to John Paul Jones.

American Naval Officer

In the lead up to the American Revolution (War of American Independence) when Congress was forming a 'Continental Navy', Jones offered his services and was commissioned as a first lieutenant on the *Alfred* in 1775. Later, as captain of the *Providence*, he advised Congress on naval regulations. In 1778, after a daring hit-and-run raid on Whitehaven, he sailed across the Solway to Kirkcudbright Bay to kidnap the Earl of Selkirk and ransom him for American captives. However the earl was not at home and the raiding party had to be content with looting the family silver.

Famous Battle

In September 1779, as commodore of a small squadron of French ships, John Paul Jones engaged his ship the *Bonhomme Richard* with the superior HMS *Serapis* and HMS *Countess of Scarborough* off Flamborough Head. After a dreadful 4-hour fight, in which Jones was injured and his ship sunk, he eventually won the battle, transferred his crew to the *Serapis* and sailed for Holland with his prisoners and booty.

John Paul Jones died in France in 1792 and his body lay in an unmarked grave for over a century. His remains were eventually taken back to the USA amid great ceremony and was finally laid to rest in the chapel crypt of the Annapolis Naval Academy in 1913.

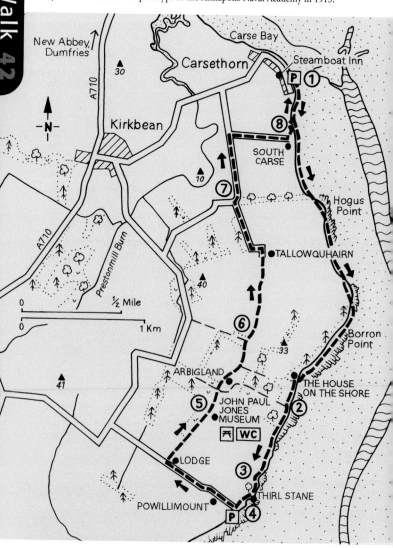

Walk 42 Directions

① From the car park at **Carsethorn** head down on to the beach and turn right. Continue walking along the shore for approximately 2 miles (3.2km). The beach at this point is sandy and may be strewn with driftwood, but if the tide is in you will be walking over more rocky ground.

Walk 42

② After you reach **The House on the Shore**, which is beside the beach on your right, the headland juts out and you should look for a track heading uphill on the right. At the top of the hill a well-defined track heads alongside a stone wall.

WHERE TO EAT AND DRINK ⓘ

The **Steamboat Inn**, just opposite the car park at Carsethorn has been trading since 1813 and, while offering up-to-the-minute comforts, still retains the atmosphere of those bygone days when immigrants left here to take the steamer to Liverpool for onward transport to the colonies. A real fire, real ales and a reputation for the best food in the district makes this a natural choice for walkers and families.

---

③ Look for a fainter track leading off to the left, which descends steeply to arrive at the beach beside a natural rock arch called the **Thirl Stane**. You can go through the arch to the sea if the tide is in, although if the tide is out on this part of the coast, the sea will be far off in the distance.

④ Continue from here along the rocks on the pebble shore and up a grassy bank until you reach a car park. Exit the car park on to a lane. Continue on the lane past **Powillimount**. Turn right when you get to a lodge house on the right-hand side and walk along the estate road to reach the cottage birthplace of John Paul Jones.

⑤ There are picnic tables here and a fascinating small **museum**. Continue along the road past the gates to **Arbigland** on to the road signed 'No vehicular traffic'. Follow the road as it turns right and along the side of some of the Arbigland Estate buildings.

⑥ When the road turns left at a cottage, go right on to a dirt track. Follow the dirt track until it emerges on to a surfaced road next to **Tallowquhairn** to your right. Take the road away from the farm, turning sharply left around some houses, then right and continue to a T-junction.

⑦ Turn right and follow this road round to the left. Follow the long straight road as far as the right turn to **South Carse**. Go along the farm road and straight through the farm steading as far as you can go, then turn left.

WHAT TO LOOK FOR ⓘ

The rocks between Hogus Point and Arbigland date from the Carboniferous era some 345 million years ago. **Fossils** in this area are well exposed and those of coral, cuttlefish, fish vertebrae, shells and tooth plates can be found. Near the beach at Powillimount look for fossilised tree ferns.

---

⑧ To return to the shore again, walk along a footpath passing a brightly coloured caravan and the rear of some cottages. Look out for a narrow track heading downhill to the right allowing access to the beach. Turn left and walk along the beach to the car park.

WHILE YOU'RE THERE ⓘ

The Victorian **Shambellie House**, just outside the village of New Abbey, contains a unique collection of costumes and is part of the National Museums of Scotland. Most of the clothes are displayed in natural settings in a series of tableaux. In the dining room is an after dinner game of carpet bowls c1905 while two women in 1920s evening dress are playing the gramophone in the library and a 1930s bride is getting dressed in the bedroom.

Walk 43

A Windy Walk to St Abb's Head

A refreshing wildlife walk along the cliffs.

•DISTANCE•	4 miles (6.4km)
•MINIMUM TIME•	1hr 30min
•ASCENT / GRADIENT•	443ft (135m) ▲▲▲
•LEVEL OF DIFFICULTY•	
•PATHS•	Clear footpaths and established tracks
•LANDSCAPE•	Dramatic cliff tops and lonely lighthouse
•SUGGESTED MAP•	aqua3 OS Explorer 346 Berwick-upon-Tweed
•START / FINISH•	Grid reference: NT 913674
•DOG FRIENDLINESS•	They'll love the fresh air, but keep on lead by cliffs
•PARKING•	At visitor centre
•PUBLIC TOILETS•	At visitor centre

BACKGROUND TO THE WALK

St Abb's Head is one of those places that people forget to visit. You only ever seem to hear it mentioned on the shipping forecast – and its name is generally followed by a rather chilly outlook – along the lines of 'north easterly five, continuous light drizzle, poor'. In fact you could be forgiven for wondering if it even exists or is simply a mysterious expanse of sea – like Dogger, Fisher or German Bight.

But St Abb's Head does exist, as you'll find out on this lovely windswept walk which will rumple your hair and leave the salty tang of the sea lingering on your lips. The dramatic cliffs, along which you walk to reach the lonely lighthouse, form an ideal home for thousands of nesting seabirds as they provide superb protection from mammalian predators. Birds you might spot on this walk include guillemots, razorbills, kittiwakes, herring gulls, shags and fulmars – as well as a few puffins.

Guillemots and razorbills are difficult to differentiate, as they're both black and white, and have an upright stance – rather like small, perky penguins. However, you should be able to spot the difference if you've got binoculars as razorbills have distinctive blunt beaks. Both birds belong to the auk family, the most famous member of which is probably the great auk, which went the way of the dodo and became extinct in 1844 – a victim of the contemporary passion for egg collecting.

Luckily no egg collector could scale these cliffs, which are precipitous and surrounded by treacherous seas. Do this walk in the nesting season (May to July) and you may well see young birds jumping off the high cliff ledge into the open sea below. Even though they can't yet fly, as their wings are little more than stubs, the baby birds are nevertheless excellent swimmers and have a better chance of survival in the water than in their nests – where they could fall prey to marauding gulls. Neither razorbills nor guillemots are particularly agile in the air, but they swim with the ease of seals, using their wings and feet to propel and steer their sleek little bodies as they fish beneath the waves.

While the steep cliffs are home to most of the seabirds round St Abb's Head, the low, flat rocks below are also used by wildlife, as they are the favoured nesting site of shags. These large black birds are almost indistinguishable from cormorants – except for the distinctive crest on their heads that gives them a quizzical appearance. They tend to fly low over the water – in contrast to the graceful fulmars that frequently soar along the cliff tops as you walk, hitching a ride on convenient currents of air.

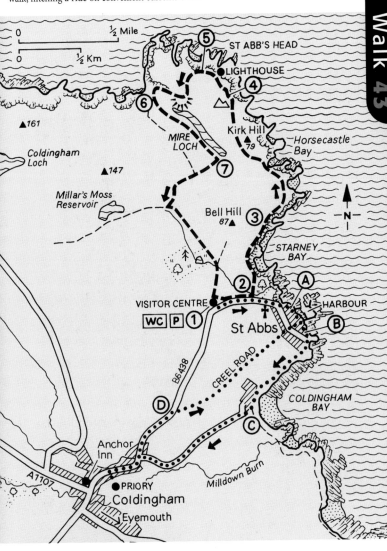

Walk 43 Directions

① From the car park, take the path that runs past the information board and the play area. Walk past the **visitor centre**, then take the footpath on the left, parallel to the

main road. At the end of the path turn left and go through a kissing gate – you'll immediately get great views of the sea.

② Follow the track, pass the sign to Starney Bay and continue, passing fields on your left-hand side. Your

track now winds around the edge of
the bay – to your right is the little
harbour at St Abbs. The track then
winds around the cliff edge, past
dramatic rock formations and
eventually to some steps.

③ Walk down the steps, then follow
the grassy track as it bears left, with
a fence on the left. Go up a slope,
over a stile and maintain direction
on the obvious grassy track. The
path soon veers away from the cliff
edge, past high ground on the right,
then runs up a short, steep slope to
a crossing of tracks.

④ Maintain direction by taking the
left-hand track which runs up a
slope. You'll soon get great views of
the **St Abb's Head lighthouse**
ahead, dramatically situated on the
cliff's edge. Continue to the
lighthouse and walk in front of the
lighthouse buildings and down to
join a tarmac road.

⑤ Follow this road which takes you
away from the cliff edge. Continue
to an obvious bend, from where
you get your first views of the

Mire Loch below. You now follow
the path downhill to the right, to
reach a cattle grid.

⑥ Turn left here to pick up the
narrow track by the loch, with the
wall on your right-hand side. It's
pretty overgrown at the start so can
be hard to find, but it soon becomes
much more obvious. Walk beside
the loch and continue until you
reach a gate.

⑦ Turn right along the wide track
and walk up to the road. Go left
now and continue to cross a cattle
grid. When you reach a bend in the
road, follow the tarmac track as it
bears left. You'll soon go through a
gate, then pass some cottages before
reaching the car park on the left-
hand side.

And on to the Village of Coldingham

A loop to St Abbs harbour and peaceful Coldingham, which is surprisingly rich in history.
See map and information panel for Walk 43

Walk 44

•DISTANCE•	2½ miles (4km)
•MINIMUM TIME•	1hr
•ASCENT / GRADIENT•	197ft (60m)
•LEVEL OF DIFFICULTY•	

Walk 44 Directions (Walk 43 option)

From Point ①, walk past the car park and along the road, following the safe footpaths on either side of the road, to pass the church. You soon reach a small **museum** on the right-hand side. Continue down to reach the pretty little harbour (Point Ⓐ) in the village of **St Abbs**, then work your way back uphill, past some small cottages, to reach **Castle Rock** guest house. Here (Point Ⓑ) follow the coastal footpath, signposted 'to Coldingham Sands'. It's a solid track, dotted with

seats so you can sit and enjoy the view. When you reach **Coldingham Bay**, bear right on the track that swings uphill. You will come out at a post-box at **St Vidas Hotel**. Take the footpath (Point Ⓒ) that runs parallel to the road and follow it into **Coldingham**. Turn left here if you want to visit the **priory** in the village, otherwise turn right towards St Abbs. At a lay-by, turn right to join the **Creel Road** (Point Ⓓ) and follow it all the way back to **St Abbs**. This path was used for well over a thousand years by local fishermen and the monks of Coldingham Priory. At the end of the path, turn left and retrace your steps to the car park.

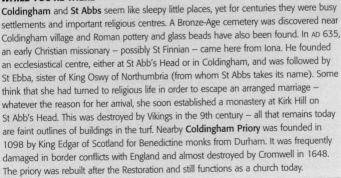

WHILE YOU'RE THERE

Coldingham and **St Abbs** seem like sleepy little places, yet for centuries they were busy settlements and important religious centres. A Bronze-Age cemetery was discovered near Coldingham village and Roman pottery and glass beads have also been found. In AD 635, an early Christian missionary – possibly St Finnian – came here from Iona. He founded an ecclesiastical centre, either at St Abb's Head or in Coldingham, and was followed by St Ebba, sister of King Oswy of Northumbria (from whom St Abbs takes its name). Some think that she had turned to religious life in order to escape an arranged marriage – whatever the reason for her arrival, she soon established a monastery at Kirk Hill on St Abb's Head. This was destroyed by Vikings in the 9th century – all that remains today are faint outlines of buildings in the turf. Nearby **Coldingham Priory** was founded in 1098 by King Edgar of Scotland for Benedictine monks from Durham. It was frequently damaged in border conflicts with England and almost destroyed by Cromwell in 1648. The priory was rebuilt after the Restoration and still functions as a church today.

Walk 45

Utopia at New Lanark

A rustic walk from a model industrial community.

•DISTANCE•	6 miles (9.7km)
•MINIMUM TIME•	3hrs
•ASCENT / GRADIENT•	476ft (145m) ▲▲▲
•LEVEL OF DIFFICULTY•	
•PATHS•	Clear riverside tracks and forest paths, few steep steps
•LANDSCAPE•	Planned industrial town and some stunning waterfalls
•SUGGESTED MAP•	aqua3 OS Explorer 335 Lanark & Tinto Hills
•START / FINISH•	Grid reference: NS 883425
•DOG FRIENDLINESS•	Good, plenty of smells by river and can mostly run free
•PARKING•	Main car park above New Lanark
•PUBLIC TOILETS•	Visitor centre (when open)

Walk 45 Directions

From the car park, walk downhill. You'll soon see the mills below you. Walk past the church and into the centre of the planned industrial village of New Lanark. This was built as a cotton-spinning centre in 1785 and is so well preserved that it is now a UNESCO World Heritage Site. It owes its fame to Welshman Robert Owen, who took over its management in 1799 and made it the focus of a revolutionary social experiment. Unlike most industrialists of his day, Owen did not allow children under ten to work in his mills – he established the world's first nursery school and ensured that all children received a rounded initial education. He disapproved of cruel treatment of his workers and refused to allow corporal punishment to be used as a form of discipline. His workers were provided with good housing, free medical care and their own co-operative store. Although Owen couldn't create Utopia, he did inspire the creation of several other model villages such as Saltaire, Port Sunlight and Bournville.

Bear left now and follow the signs to the Scottish Wildlife Trust centre. Now turn up the stone steps on the left, following the signs to the **Falls of Clyde**. Follow the path, then go down some steps to reach the weir, where there's a lookout point. Now continue to follow the path. You'll eventually pass **Bonnington Power Station** on your right, where the path divides. Take the right-hand path, which begins to climb and takes you into woodland and up some steps. You'll soon come to **Corra Linn waterfall**, where there's another lookout point. There's a

---

WHILE YOU'RE THERE ℹ

The ruins of Corra Castle, built in the 13th century, are home to a colony of **Natterer's bat**. These medium-sized bats are found throughout Britain. In winter they tend to hibernate in caves and mines, while in summer they prefer to roost in old stone buildings and barns. Their limbs have a slight pink tinge, giving rise to the bats' nickname of the 'red-armed bat'.

plaque here explaining how the falls inspired painters such as Turner and Moore, as well as the poet Wordsworth, who visited the falls in 1802 with his sister Dorothy and friend Samuel Taylor Coleridge. Your path then continues to the right, signposted 'Bonnington Linn ¾ mile'.

Go up some more steps and follow the wide track until you go under a double line of pylons. Just after this is an area that is often fenced off to protect breeding peregrines – their nest site is surveyed by cameras until the young have left the nest. The path is obvious though so you can't go wrong – and you follow it until you reach the large new bridge. Cross over the bridge, then turn right into the **Falls of Clyde Wildlife Reserve**. Walk through the reserve until you come to a crossing of paths at which you turn right, then walk over a small bridge. Walk underneath the double line of pylons again, then bear right at the gate.

> ### WHERE TO EAT AND DRINK ⓘ
> There's a self-service **café** in the village where you can get baked potatoes with various fillings, sandwiches, cakes and hot drinks. On fine days you can buy ice creams from a **kiosk** in the village and you can also buy tooth-rotting fudge from the old-fashioned **village store**.

You'll come to **Corra Castle**, hidden away on the right-hand side. It's very atmospheric and overgrown with ivy – but you mustn't go in as you could disturb the bats (see While You're There). Now continue walking by the river, go over a small footbridge then follow the wide path that leads through the woods. When you meet another path, turn right and you'll soon come to some houses on your left-hand side. When you reach the road turn right (take care as there's no pavement), then go right again to walk over the old bridge. This brings you into a cul de sac, where you go through the gate on the right-hand side – it looks as if you are going into someone's drive but it's signed 'Clyde Walkway'.

Walk past the stables and down to the river. Go through a metal gate to reach a **water treatment works** and walk up the steps beside it. Walk past a stile on your left and continue on the main track, following the signs for the Clyde Walkway. Pass a house on the right-hand side, then follow the path that leads down to the right (there's a fingerpost but the finger had been broken off when I was there). Your path now zig-zags downhill to reach the river. When you come to the water's edge turn left, go over a footbridge and follow the wide forest track. You'll go down some steps, close to the river again, then up a flight of stairs and over a bridge. Just after this you'll get some great views of the mills again. Follow the path as it winds back on to the road, then turn right and walk down the hill and back into **New Lanark**. Turn left at the church and walk back to the car park.

> ### WHAT TO LOOK FOR ⓘ
> **Peregrines** nest near the Corra Linn Falls from April to June and high-powered telescopes have been set up to allow you to view their nest without disturbing the birds. They are a protected species and there are only around 800 pairs in Scotland. Sadly, they are threatened by egg collectors, shooting and poisoning. Peregrines are noted for their steep dive to catch their prey, at speeds of up to 120mph (193kph).

Away on the Merrick

Follow in the cycle tracks of Davie Bell, the original mountain biker.

•DISTANCE•	9 miles (14.5km)
•MINIMUM TIME•	5hrs
•ASCENT / GRADIENT•	2,339ft (713m) ▲▲▲
•LEVEL OF DIFFICULTY•	
•PATHS•	Hill tracks, section to Loch Enoch can be very boggy, 1 stile
•LANDSCAPE•	Hills, lochs and trees
•SUGGESTED MAP•	aqua3 OS Explorer 318 Galloway Forest North
•START / FINISH•	Grid reference: NX 415804
•DOG FRIENDLINESS•	Keep on lead at lambing time and near stock
•PARKING•	Bruce's Stone car park
•PUBLIC TOILETS•	At car park

BACKGROUND TO THE WALK

A 1940s photograph shows a group of young men gathered round the cairn at the summit of the Merrick, south west Scotland's highest mountain. Nothing unusual there, except for the fact that they all have bicycles. It's an amazing record of the successful outcome of a challenge from a newspaper editor and a tribute to one of Ayrshire's cycling pioneers.

The Highwayman

David E T Bell (1907–65) was born and educated in Dumfries, then he moved to Ayr where he worked as a gardener. Health and fitness were his passions and when he was introduced to cycling he saw it as a means to achieve both. But Davie Bell was much more than a sportsman. He was a keen local historian and an outdoor man with an eye for nature. He had a wonderfully descriptive writing style, which ensured that thousands followed his adventures as 'The Highwayman' in his weekly column in the *Ayrshire Post*.

One week the *Post* published a letter from a reader who had gone to the summit of Merrick on a pony. He closed his correspondence with the challenge, 'It only remains for someone to make the ascent on a bicycle.' The Highwayman rose to the bait and, with four friends, set off through the mist covered Minnoch Valley heading for Merrick. Riding and walking, sometimes using a sling to carry their bikes, they progressed slowly up the hill, some of them collapsing and gasping for breath, while Davie's pal, Harry Fairbairn kept up a constant monologue, 'Jings this is smashing. I never saw anything like this.' Eventually they reached the summit and took a photograph to record the feat. Then followed the descent of the sloping ridge of the Neive of the Spit to Ben Yellery 'one hectic mile of crashing and bumping that smashed my back mudguard.' From Ben Yellery they covered another 2,000ft (610m) at a slower pace to finally descend through granite boulders to Loch Trool.

Davie Bell continued with his passion for 'rough stuff' for the rest of his life, making journeys to remote bothies like Back Hill of Bush or hauling his bike to the summit of the rocky island of Ailsa Craig in the Firth of Clyde. On each journey he took his readers with him, producing a weekly column for 30 years. When he died in 1965 subscriptions poured in from friends and admirers and a memorial cairn was erected at Rowantree Toll on the Straiton to Newton Stewart road.

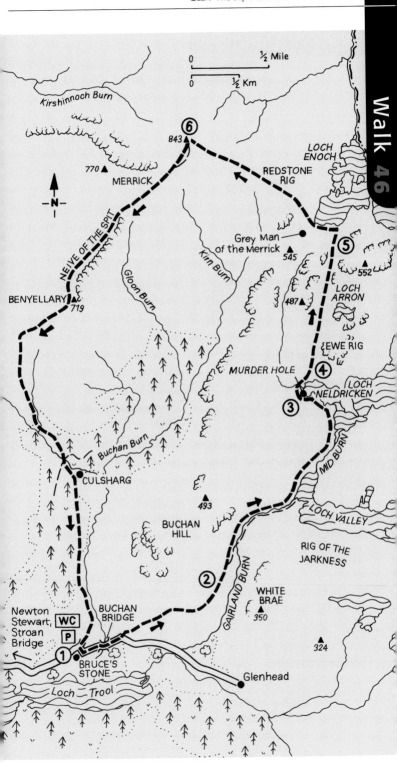

Kirshinnoch Burn

⑥ 843

LOCH ENOCH

770 ▲

MERRICK

REDSTONE RIG

–N–

Grey Man of the Merrick ● 545

⑤

552 ▲

NEIVE OF THE SPIT

Gloon Burn

Kirn Burn

BENYELLARY ▲ 719

487 ▲

LOCH ARRON

EWE RIG

MURDER HOLE

④

Buchan Burn

③

LOCH NELDRICKEN

CULSHARG

MID BURN

493 ▲

BUCHAN HILL

LOCH VALLEY

RIG OF THE JARKNESS

②

GAIRLAND BURN

WHITE BRAE 350 ▲

324 ▲

Newton Stewart, Stroan Bridge

WC

P

BUCHAN BRIDGE

①

BRUCE'S STONE

Glenhead

Loch Trool

Walk 46

Walk 46 Directions

① From the car park at **Bruce's Stone** head east along the narrow road, across the **Buchan Bridge**. Continue a short distance then turn left and go uphill to cross a stile. Follow the path along the wall, then veer right and head uphill to rejoin the wall. Go through a gate and turn right on to a path. Follow this up the valley of the **Gairland Burn** with **Buchan Hill** on your left.

> **WHAT TO LOOK FOR** ℹ
> From the corner of Loch Enoch come back a little way to the south west, heading towards the summit of Buchan Hill and look for a large outcrop called the **Grey Man of the Merrick**. It's a well-known landmark in these hills and resembles the face of a man.

② To your left is the ridge of Buchan Hill and to the right is White Brae and to the farside of that the Rig of the Jarkness. Do not cross the Gairland but keep going on the path to reach **Loch Valley**, skirting it to the west and then continue beside the **Mid Burn** to reach **Loch Neldricken**.

③ Head for the far west corner of the loch to find the infamous **Murder Hole** featured by S R Crockett in his novel *The Raiders* (1894). The story is based on a local legend that unwary travellers were robbed on these hills and their bodies disposed of in the loch.

④ From the Murder Hole head north, crossing a burn and then a wall. Pass to the east of the **Ewe Rig** and tiny **Loch Arron** and eventually reach the south side of **Loch Enoch**. Don't worry if the track vanishes or becomes indistinct, just keep heading north and you'll eventually reach the loch.

⑤ As you approach Loch Enoch you will see the outline of Mullwarchar beyond it and to the right. When you reach the loch go left and cross another wall. The slope in front of you is the **Redstone Rig** and although you have 1,000ft (305m) to climb it is

> **WHERE TO EAT AND DRINK** ℹ
> Well this is the Galloway Hills and a pretty remote area. Not only is a picnic a good idea but by the time you've conquered Merrick you will feel in need of sustenance. The other options include the **Stroan Bridge Visitor Centre**, which has a tea room, and **The House O' Hill** at Bargrennan.

not particularly taxing.

⑥ From the summit cairn of **Merrick** head downhill towards a narrow ridge called the **Neive of the Spit** to reach the summit of **Benyellary**, the Hill of the Eagle. From here follow the footpath downhill beside a dry-stone wall then turn left and keep going downhill, into the forest, to reach the bothy at **Culsharg**. From there continue downhill to return to the

> **WHILE YOU'RE THERE** ℹ
> Take a trip to **Whithorn** where Christianity first arrived in Scotland towards the end of the 4th century. This is where St Ninian founded his early church Candida Casa, the White House, from where the name Whithorn comes. Once a popular place of pilgrimage, and a thriving community until pilgrimages were banned under pain of death after the Reformation, it is once again receiving attention because of recent archaeological discoveries. You can visit the interpretation centre, the dig and the old priory.

A Trail Through the Sallochy Woods

A gentle stroll by the bonnie banks of Loch Lomond.

•DISTANCE•	2 miles (3.2km)
•MINIMUM TIME•	2hrs 30min
•ASCENT / GRADIENT•	131ft (40m) ▲ ▲ ▲
•LEVEL OF DIFFICULTY•	
•PATHS•	West Highland Way, forest trail and forest road
•LANDSCAPE•	Loch, hills and woodland
•SUGGESTED MAP•	aqua3 OS Explorer 364 Loch Lomond North
•START / FINISH•	Grid reference: NS 380957
•DOG FRIENDLINESS•	Suitable for dogs
•PARKING•	Sallochy Woods car park
•PUBLIC TOILETS•	None on route

BACKGROUND TO THE WALK

One of Scotland's best-known songs, *The Bonnie Banks of Loch Lomond*, was reputedly written by a soldier of Prince Charles Edward Stuart's army during the Jacobite rising of 1745. During the long, slow retreat from Derby the soldier was captured and taken to Carlisle Castle and it was here that he wrote the song for his love, while languishing in prison awaiting execution. It tells of their joy in each other's company on the banks of Loch Lomond and how she would make the lonely journey home to Scotland by the 'high road'. Meanwhile his soul would be instantly transported at the moment of death back to his beloved loch along the 'low road' of the underworld and reach there before her. It's a poignant song of love and parting and a nostalgic remembrance of a landscape that the soldier will never see again in life.

Loch Lomond

Loch Lomond is the largest fresh water lake in Britain. It is 24 miles (38.6km) long, 5 miles (8km) wide and, at its deepest point is 623ft (190m) deep. Within its banks are approximately 38 islands, some of which are inhabited while others form sanctuaries for birds and wildlife. Most of them are in private ownership and not open to visitors. Inchcailloch is part of the National Nature Reserve and Bucinch and Ceardach are National Trust for Scotland properties. They can be visited and in summer a ferry and mail boat operate a regular passenger service from the boatyard at Balmaha, allowing island exploration and the opportunity to lunch at the Inchmurrin Hotel on Inchmurrin.

Geological Fault

The loch straddles the Highland Boundary Fault, a fracture caused by movement of the earth's crust millions of years ago, and the geological differences between Highland and Lowland Scotland are clearly visible from its banks. Here the fault runs from Conic Hill on the south east shore and through the islands of Inchcailloch, Torrinch, Creinch and Inchmurrin.

Forest Park

Most visitors rush up the busy A82 along the west side of Loch Lomond, but on the more secluded eastern shore there is a largely unspoilt area of tranquillity and beauty, even in the height of summer. The diverse woods here are part of the Queen Elizabeth Forest Park and contain walking and nature trails and isolated picnic spots. The variety of animals and plants which can be found is staggering. Over a quarter of the plants that flourish in Britain can be found around the loch. You may well spot the rare capercaillie (it's the size of a turkey), ptarmigan or even a golden eagle. On Inchcailloch white fallow deer have been spotted in the past. While on Inchconnacan you might encounter a wallaby. They were transported here from the Australian outback some years ago, by Lady Arran.

Walk 47 **Directions**

① From the car park head towards the entrance on to the main road. Go right on to a track beside the starting post to the **Sallochy Trail**. Cross the road with care and continue along the trail on the other side. This runs alongside some woodland which you should keep on your your right-hand side. Continue and, when the path eventually forks, keep right and go into the wood following the obvious waymarker posts.

WHILE YOU'RE THERE ⓘ

Head for **Loch Lomond Shores** a new gateway visitor attraction situated at Balloch. Within Drumkinnon Tower are viewing galleries and shops as well as two informative shows and a street theatre troupe. Here you can journey with a young otter through some of the myths and legends of the loch or watch and listen as the scenery becomes the backdrop to the story behind the song.

② The trail goes through the wood and passes into the ruined 19th-century farm steading of **Wester Sallochy** which the Forestry Commission has now cleared of trees. Several buildings can be seen and its worth spending some time investigating these old ruins and trying to imagine life in those times. When you have finished, circle the buildings to the left and follow the well-worn trail until it ends at a T-junction beside a waymarker post. Turn right on to the forest road here.

③ Follow the forest road for about ½ mile (800m) to reach a gate just before the junction with the main road. Cross the gate, then cross the main road and turn right. Look carefully for a faint track running through the woods to your left.

④ Follow the faint track back towards the loch (if you miss the track then enter the wood at any point and head west towards the loch). When the track intersects with a well-surfaced footpath turn right. You are now on the **West Highland Way**. Follow the waymarkers, keeping on the main path and ignoring any subsidiary tracks branching off it.

WHAT TO LOOK FOR ⓘ

Large **oak trees** remain from when these woods were used to provide a constant supply of timber. They were under a coppice system of management throughout the 18th and 19th centuries which divided the area into a series of sections or 'hags'. Each hag was felled every 24 years but the best 400 trees would be left another 24 years and eight of these were spared to go on growing.

WHERE TO EAT AND DRINK ⓘ

Try the **tea room** of the garden centre on the shores of the loch at Balmaha. Here you'll find friendly service, food that is hot, tasty and nourishing and some dreadfully fattening cakes. Alternatively eat in one of several cafés and restaurants at **Loch Lomond Shores** where, as well as superb views, you'll find everything from snacks to seafood.

⑤ Follow the path uphill through a rocky section and then, as it levels off, through a wood. There is some boggy ground here but strategically placed duckboards make the going easier. Eventually the trail passes through the **Sallochy Woods** car park returning you to the start.

Walk 48

Grey Mare's Tail and Mamore Lodge

A waterfall, a shooting lodge and a ramble down the West Highland Way.

•DISTANCE•	3½ miles (5.7km)
•MINIMUM TIME•	2hrs 15min
•ASCENT / GRADIENT•	984ft (300m) ▲▲▲
•LEVEL OF DIFFICULTY•	
•PATHS•	Well-made paths, one steep, rough ascent, no stiles
•LANDSCAPE•	Birchwoods leading to long views along Loch Leven
•SUGGESTED MAP•	aqua3 OS Explorer 384 Glen Coe & Glen Etive or 392 Ben Nevis & Fort William
•START / FINISH•	Grid reference: NN 187622
•DOG FRIENDLINESS•	Off lead unless sheep near by
•PARKING•	Grey Mare's Tail car park, Kinlochleven
•PUBLIC TOILETS•	Kinlochleven, at bridge over River Leven

BACKGROUND TO THE WALK

Aluminium is a very common metal: around eight per cent of the earth's crust is made up of it. It's very reactive, which means that it's extremely difficult to extract the aluminium atoms out of the ore called bauxite. There is no chemical method for this process. Instead, it's done by dissolving the ore in molten cryolite (a fluoride mineral) and applying vast quantities of electricity.

As a result, aluminium processing doesn't take place where you find the bauxite, but where you find the electricity, with lots of water coming down steep hillsides, and a deep-water harbour at the bottom, such as Kinlochleven.

The village of Kinlochleven was built around the smelter. Two lochs above have been dammed for hydro-electricity, and six huge pipes bring the water down from a control station above the Devil's Staircase footpath.

Pipeline or Path

A pipeline on the OS Landranger map is a dotted line, rather like a path. And it may be that the path of this walk happened by mistake, as walkers mistook the pipeline for a path, walked along it and so created the path that they thought was there in the first place. The pipeline path leads from the outflow of Loch Eilde Mor, around the head of Loch Leven along the 1,100ft (335m) contour, giving superb views towards the Pap of Glencoe and the loch's foot. Eventually, it carries Loch Eilde's water to the Blackwater Reservoir.

Why has the water from Loch Eilde been taken all the way round this hillside to the Blackwater Reservoir, instead of straight down to the turbines where it's actually needed? You need to glance across the valley at the six descending pipes for the answer. At the foot of those huge reinforced pipes the water is under 30 tons per square foot (300 tonnes/sq m) of pressure. A second such set from Loch Eilde would cost far more than the much longer, unpressurised pipe to the other reservoir. Besides, we wouldn't have ended up with this fine contour-line walk.

The Kinlochmore smelter started as one of the largest in the world, but by the end of the 1900s it was the world's smallest. It closed in 2000, although its turbines continue to generate electricity, which is now diverted to the smelter at Fort William or into the National Grid. The smelter had been the reason for Kinlochleven, and its main employer. Projects to keep Kinlochleven alive include the fine, newly constructed path system, the visitor centre and the Atlas Brewery on the site where carbon electrical connectors were once made.

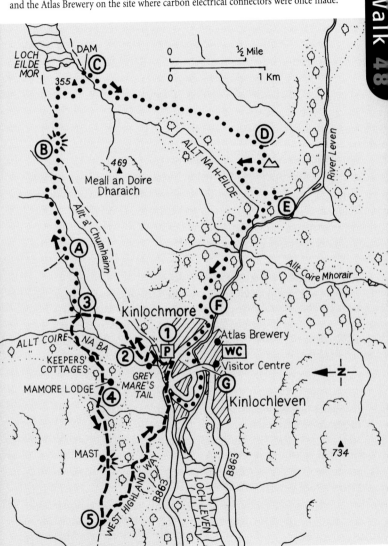

Walk 48 Directions

① A smooth gravel path leads up out of the car park to multicoloured waymarks pointing left. The path rises to a view through trees of the **Grey Mare's Tail waterfall**, then descends to a footbridge. Here turn left (blue waymarker) to visit the foot of the spectacular waterfall, then return to take the path on the

Walk 48

right (white, yellow and green waymarker). Follow the stream up for 100yds (91m), then turn left at a waymarker. The path, quite steep and loose, zig-zags up through birches to more open ground.

② Here the path forks. Take the right-hand branch, with a yellow and green waymarker, to pass under power lines. The path follows the crest of a heathery spur, then bends left to cross two streams. Immediately after the second stream is another junction.

> **WHILE YOU'RE THERE** ℹ
> The **Aluminium Story Visitor Centre** at Kinlochleven is worth a quick visit, although its displays are entirely audio-visual. Alternatively, you could tour the **Atlas Brewery**, in a disused part of the aluminium works (after 5:30PM).

③ The confusing waymarker here has eight arrows in four colours. Turn left, following a white arrow slightly downhill, to cross a footbridge above a waterfall and red granite rocks. The path leads up under birches. Here the ground cover includes the aromatic bog myrtle, which can be used to discourage midges, though it is less effective than a chemical repellent. When the path reaches a track, turn left (white arrow). Below the track is a tin deer used by stalkers for target practice: it's more convenient than the real thing as it doesn't wander off just when you're creeping up on it. A signed footpath bypasses the **Keepers' Cottages** on the left, then rejoins the track beyond, to a junction above **Mamore Lodge**.

④ Keep ahead, above the lodge, climbing gently past two tin huts, self-catering accommodation

> **WHERE TO EAT AND DRINK** ℹ
> The **Tailrace Inn**, in Kinlochleven, is a service station on the West Highland Way. They welcome children (if having a meal) and dogs on the benches outside. In summer, you won't get through an evening without a rousing chorus of *Bonnie Banks of Loch Lomond*. Try the Atlas Brewery's 'Wayfarer' ale, brewed for thirsty West Highland Way walkers.

labelled 'stable' and 'bothy'. At the high point of the track there is a TV mast on the right, a bench on the left and a view along Loch Leven ahead. The track descends gently, with slabs of whitish quartzite above. The wide path of the **West Highland Way** (WHW) can be seen below and gradually rises to join the track, with a large waymarker planted in a cairn.

⑤ Turn left down the West Highland Way path, which drops into the woods below. Watch out for a junction where the main path seems to double back to the right; take the smaller path, continuing ahead with a WHW waymarker. After crossing the tarred access track of **Mamore Lodge**, the path fords a small stream to reach the village. Turn left along the pavement and fork left into **Wades Road** to regain the car park.

> **WHAT TO LOOK FOR** ℹ
> The view down the length of Loch Leven, which is such a feature of Walks 48 and 49, ends on the left with a small pointed mountain. Though only 2,434ft (742m) high, it's one of Scotland's sharpest peaks outside Skye. '**Sgurr na Ciche**' describes its shape exactly: less explicit English translates it as the 'Pap' of Glencoe. Alan Breck and Davie Balfour sheltered high on its slopes in Robert Louis Stevenson's classic Highland novel *Kidnapped*.

Aluminium Landscape Above Kinlochleven

A sea loch, a mountain loch and a pipeline path above deep wooded glens.
See map and information panel for Walk 48

·DISTANCE·	6¾ miles (10.9km)
·MINIMUM TIME·	3hrs 45min
·ASCENT / GRADIENT·	1,400ft (426m) ▲▲▲
·LEVEL OF DIFFICULTY·	

Walk 49 Directions (Walk 48 option)

Follow Walk 48 up to Point ③. At this junction turn right, following a yellow waymarker. The path climbs beside a stream, then bends right to cross it and another stream, to reach a track (Point Ⓐ). A continuation path rises briefly above the track then rejoins it.

Follow the track uphill towards a wide pass. Just before it, a path on the right is a short-cut back to Kinlochleven. At the pass (Point Ⓑ) is a view ahead along Loch Eilde Mor, the Big Loch of the Hind.

Descend for ¼ mile (400m) to a path forking off on the right. After 220yds (201m), bend right. A smaller path ahead goes only to the loch foot, while the main path leads to the right of a knoll to a dam over the **Allt na h-Eilde** (Point Ⓒ).

Turn right on to a rough and sometimes soggy track. This follows a concrete pipeline across the hill face, high above Kinlochleven, with fine views. In the pipeline below, look out for a rusty metal item like a tea-strainer on a stick – this is a pressure release valve. After 1¼ miles (2km), the path drops below the pipeline and, in another 200yds (183m), a cairn marks a steep path descending on the right (Point Ⓓ).

As you set off downhill, to the left you should see the Crowberry Tower on distant Buachaille Etive Mor, outlined against the sky. The path becomes very rough as it enters the wood, but then passes through a wall gap and rises slightly to join another path (Point Ⓔ). Bear right on this path to the edge of **Kinlochleven** (Point Ⓕ).

The track ahead has a West Highland Way marker. Shortly it becomes a street; look for the tarred path on the left where the WHW turns back to the riverside. You pass the tailrace at the former smelter to the road bridge (Point Ⓖ). You can turn up right into Kinlochleven here. For a longer walk, continue under the bridge to a riverside path. It bends right, past black garages, to an earth path upstream alongside the **Allt Coire na Ba**. A new path continues under hazels; where it ends, a few steps ahead you cross the **B863** into **Wade Road**. This leads to the car park.

Walk 50

Waterfalls and Wade's Walk

A sheltered forest ramble high above Loch Linnhe.

•DISTANCE•	2¾ miles (4.4km)
•MINIMUM TIME•	1hr 30min
•ASCENT / GRADIENT•	600ft (183m) ▲ ▲ ▲
•LEVEL OF DIFFICULTY•	
•PATHS•	Well-made paths, forest tracks, no stiles
•LANDSCAPE•	Plantation and semi-wild forest
•SUGGESTED MAP•	aqua3 OS Explorer 384 Glen Coe & Glen Etive
•START / FINISH•	Grid reference: NN 029634
•DOG FRIENDLINESS•	Off lead in forest
•PARKING•	Forest Enterprise picnic place at road end, behind Inchree
•PUBLIC TOILETS•	Corran Ferry – bypass ferry queue and turn left into car park

Walk 50 Directions

At the bottom corner of the car park is a well-built path marked by a white waymarker. A field on its right gives views out across Loch Linnhe until it crosses a footbridge to enter woodland. The path runs gently uphill, through birchwoods with clearings of heather and grass. The **Inchree waterfalls** appear ahead, falling through a gorge lined with rhododendron.

There are seven waterfalls, though only the top three are visible from here. They are particularly fine after heavy rain, when spray drifts out above the treetops. The path turns uphill, staying about 100yds (91m)

from the falls, but with fine views of them, particularly from two viewpoint spurs on the right. Where the path is carved into the hillside, it shows the underlying rock, which is lumpy white quartzite. This is the same rock that gives a whitish appearance to the tops of the hills above Glen Nevis.

Above the second viewpoint, the path bends left. Here a small path runs ahead through boggy ground. This is aiming for the top of the upper fall, but it isn't recommended as the rocks alongside the fall are unsafe (wet quartzite is slippery) and you don't actually get a better view of the water.

Not far above, the path runs up to a forest road. Turn left, signed 'Car Park'. Open heather above the track is being colonised by birch and pine, and also by larch seeding itself out of the plantations below. At a junction, the downward path, which is a short-cut back to the car park, has red-and-white waymarkers. Your route turns uphill to the right, with a red waymarker.